Miniature
Landscape Modelling

Miniature
Landscape Modelling

JOHN H. AHERN

MODEL & ALLIED PUBLICATIONS
ARGUS BOOKS LIMITED
14 St James Road, Watford,
Herts., England

Model and Allied Publications
Argus Books Limited
14 St James Road, Watford,
Herts., England

First Published 1954
Second Edition 1955
Third Edition 1962
Second Impression 1968
Third Impression 1970
Fourth Impression 1971
Fifth Impression 1973
Sixth Impression 1975
Seventh Impression 1976
Eighth Impression 1979

© Argus Books Ltd, 1976

ISBN 0 85242 684 4

Printed by A. Wheaton & Co. Ltd., Exeter

Contents

Note to this Edition

This book was first published in 1954, but remains today one of the finest and most popular works on the subject, a steady best seller. The late John H. Ahern wrote the book long before the current ranges of scenic modelling accessories became available through hobby shops. The modern reader now has the added facility of using commercially available scenic materials—surface coverings, model trees, modelling plaster, etc—but the basic principles remain unchanged. At a time of greatly increased costs, even in the modelling hobby, it can, in fact, be cheaper to follow the simple basic methods for such tasks as afforestation and ground treatment rather than purchase special modelling items. Some of the commercial items mentioned in the text may be difficult to find under the brand names quoted, but alternatives are available (eg, Polyfilla or Artex)! John Ahern's Madder Valley Railway, illustrated in this book, may now be seen at the Pendon Museum, Berkshire.

Introduction

THIS book is an attempt to describe concisely and in straight-forward language the methods usually employed in scenic modelling. I have endeavoured to keep in mind throughout that the majority of readers will be disposed to approach the subject from the point of view of the craftsman rather than that of the artist. I have therefore treated the subject as essentially a branch of modelling, but where aesthetic considerations have arisen, as is to a certain extent unavoidable by the nature of the case, it has seemed better to be, if anything, over explicit, and to say too much rather than risk leaving the reader in doubt on any point.

It is hoped that the book will prove of practical value to all who undertake scenic modelling for any purpose, but I have felt obliged to exclude from my survey the special requirements of the film studio, which constitute a distinct and separate subject with in many respects a different technique.

The present-day uses of scenic modelling are very numerous. In this, as in many other things, the war has no doubt stimulated ingenuity and some of the most interesting work which has come to my knowledge was produced by Army modelling units for instructional purposes and in connection with military and aerial operations. A sound knowledge of the craft is of great value to the architect and to the planning authority, to the museum and exhibition worker, and to the commercial display expert. And, of course, one can do it just for the fun of the thing, which in many ways may be considered best of all. Certain notable applications of scenic modelling readily come to mind and serve to emphasise the diversity and adaptability of the subject. On one hand we may recall the fine museum exhibits, designed to illustrate the formation of geological strata and kindred subjects, and on the other the window display sets which have been built to the order of travel agencies, and similar bodies, to exhibit the attractions of holiday resorts.

It must be admitted that in the following pages I seem to have addressed myself more particularly to the railway modeller, but that was almost unavoidable since I am in the first place a railway modeller myself. I venture to think that it does not in any way diminish the value of the book for those who practise the craft for other purposes.

This introductory note may conclude with a remark touching on the general approach to the subject. People who are quite new to scenic work, but who have acquired considerable experience of other forms of modelling, may be inclined to view the subject in much the same frame of mind as if they were preparing to construct, say, a locomotive, or some other example of miniature engineering. They may be disposed by their training to attach excessive value to detail and precision workmanship. Now scenic modelling should be a comparatively lighthearted business and a bolder and broader approach is indicated ; it is the general effect of the whole which matters and not the accuracy and precision of any detail. This is in fact a case where it can be *literally* true that one is unable to see the wood for the trees.

Preface for Railway Modellers

S OME people may take the view that a model railway should be an end in itself and require no setting of hills, trees, rivers, and the like. They may even maintain that such etceteras detract from the special kind of beauty which belongs to well planned and laid trackwork, but the writer's experience suggests that a model railway draws much life and vitality from being related to a countryside, and since no real railway has ever been known to run in a void it is difficult to see why a model one should.

The impression produced on non-railway-minded visitors is also worthy of consideration. Their interest and enthusiasm is more likely to be aroused if the setting is natural and attractive, and those who cannot see the point in a model railway, and cannot understand why anyone should want to build one, may be captivated by minia-ture villages, farms, and rivers.

Some of the American workers in the smaller scales seem to have carried this art of scenic modelling further than most of us have here, with a bolder use of baseboard material and scenic features, and there is one aspect of their work which should be brought to the notice of readers in this country. They have escaped from the convention of the flat tabletop baseboard which is still very much in evidence over here. It is not that our model railways are necessarily quite flat but that the hills manage to look exactly and precisely what they are : structures erected on a flat surface, like the Mappin Terraces in the Regent's Park Zoo in London. But nature is not like that at all and in the following pages it is hoped to demonstrate the attractiveness of a less formal and less " suburban " type of countryside. Perhaps the following pages may convey to the reader some hints as to how he may infuse that vitality and life into his miniature world which is the soul of good railway modelling.

The mechanical and the scenic aspects of railway modelling are in many ways complementary : you provide the railway with a " countryside " and that at once suggests lines of thought for future extensions and modifications of the layout. These in turn may open the way to new scenic features, and so the process continues. If there is no countryside with its associations to stimulate the imagination the whole thing may in time become cold and fixed ; the builder's imagination refuses to produce anything new.

Scenic modelling is a very wide interest, and can be approached in many different ways. It is certainly all to the good if the reader has a liking for maps. (The writer has been accumulating maps of all descriptions on one excuse and another almost as long as he can remember.) Any knowledge the reader may have acquired of map reading, of surveying, of the habits of rivers and other waterways, even of geology, will provide inspiration in scenic modelling.

CHAPTER ONE

Baseboards and Substructure

ALTHOUGH the subject of this book is landscape and scenery it is advisable to devote a chapter to the essential foundation of baseboards and substructure, or trestling, for the success of all subsequent work depends in some degree on a sound and suitable foundation, and the builder's intentions in the matter of scenery may have some influence on the form it will take. The erection of model railway baseboards is not a very difficult undertaking and anyone who can use a saw and a screwdriver with ordinary competence should be capable of doing all that is necessary without " professional " assistance. Yet ve find that people who are perfectly self-reliant in most other respects seem to think that they must secure the services of a carpenter for this. As a matter of fact a regular carpenter's job is hardly to be recommended. It will be too perfect, and inflexible, and one will never have the courage to pull bits down and make alterations when the need arises on some future occasion. It is better, if possible, to do this work yourself because then you will not have that respect for it which you would probably develop for a professional job, for which money had been paid. You will feel yourself master of the situation, in fact.

The writer has found that a rather exaggerated idea seems to prevail as to the strength and solidity required in the under-baseboard structure. Some writers have advocated trestle legs of 3 in. by 2 in. timber and while there is no doubt that a really substantial structure is very nice it is unnecessary to go to such lengths as this if the work is carried out intelligently, not to mention that it will make the job quite unnecessarily expensive. The writer has never used anything for the trestles, or for any part of the under-baseboard framework, except ordinary 2 in. by 1 in. battening, which finishes about 1¼ in. by ¼ in. and this is probably the easiest material to obtain. It has never given any trouble in years of use, in spite of frequent alterations and re-constructions, and it is easier than heavier stuff to transport, handle, and work. Fig. 1 illustrates the general form of the substructure used by the writer, and Fig. 2 shows the various parts separated. No halved or mortised and tenoned joints are used. The trestles are made by screwing together four pieces of wood (two up-

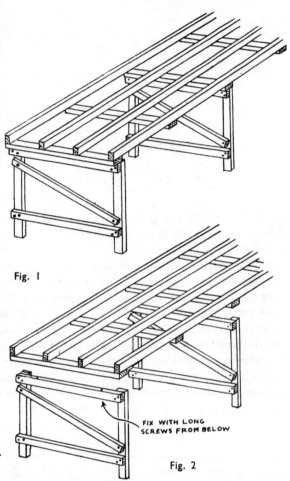

Fig. 1

FIX WITH LONG
SCREWS FROM BELOW

Fig. 2

rights and upper and lower horizontal members) with 1½ in. No. 8 woodscrews, and adding a diagonal brace. The diagonal need not be made of the same 2 in. by 1 in. stuff; almost any odd material, such as pieces from broken-up orange boxes will serve provided it is reasonably sound. It is as well to start by making up a number of these trestles, the width being governed by that of the baseboards, and the height by the opinion of the builder. The writer makes his trestles 3 ft. high, which gives an average base-board height of 3 ft. 3 in. or 3 ft. 4 in. Experience suggests that this is on the low side for a person of average height; the average base-board height could, with advantage, be about 4 ft. above the floor.

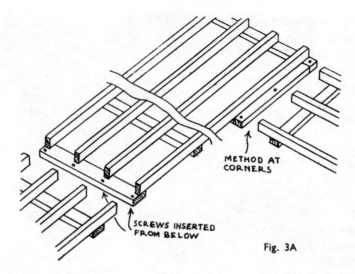

METHOD AT
CORNERS

SCREWS INSERTED
FROM BELOW

Fig. 3A

The trestles should all be the same height, even if the floor is not level. It is simpler and more positive to level the baseboard after the structure has been erected by inserting packing under the feet where necessary, than to attempt to do it by varying the height of the trestles. A carpenter's spirit-level will be required for levelling.

The framework for the baseboard sections can be made from the same 2 in. by 1 in. battening as the trestles, as shown in Figs. 1 and 2. It is suggested that the baseboards should usually be made in sections

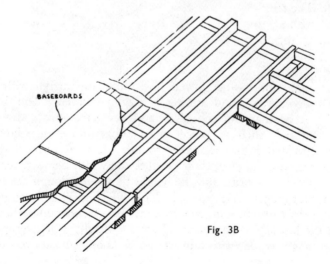

BASEBOARDS

Fig. 3B

An example of baseboard substructure, built in accordance with the
author's methods.

Another example of timber substructure, showing the arrangement
employed for dealing with a corner. On the extreme right the baseboard
swings forward to clear a chimney breast. Notice how a short section
of one of the longitudinal members has been cut away to clear the course
of a river. Information on this will be found in Chapter IV.

not more than 9 ft. long. The reason is that in case of need they should be sufficiently portable to be moved complete to a new site : an important consideration for those who may be faced with the prospect of a move at some time. The method of joining adjacent sections will be clear from Fig. 3, A and B. The transverse member at one end of each section is fitted so that half its width projects and forms a support for the ends of the longitudinal members of the next section. It is advisable to insert the fixing screws from *below* so that the sections can be taken apart, if necessary, without interfering with the baseboards which will in due course be placed on top.

The trestles are secured to the baseboards with $2\frac{1}{2}$ in. No. 8 screws, which are passed up from below through $\frac{3}{16}$ in. holes drilled in the crossmembers. It is useful to know, by the way, that a $\frac{3}{16}$ in. hole gives exactly the correct clearance for a No. 8 screw. How the baseboard sections are to be got into position on top of the trestles may require a little thought if the worker is alone and cannot call on anyone for help. It is advisable to start by finding a small table of about the same height as the trestles. Failing a suitable table a couple of packing cases or a cabin trunk would serve. One end of the baseboard is hoisted up on the table, or other temporary support. The other end is lifted and a trestle is placed in position underneath it. It will " stay put " sufficiently well to enable a screw to be driven in from below, and as soon as one screw is in place the erection will not collapse and further screws, and trestles, can be added at leisure. When a second trestle has been secured in place the temporary support can be removed.

In cases where a baseboard section can be cut to length so that it is an exact fit between the walls of a room no further support or reinforcement should be necessary. No endways movement can take place because the baseboard is wedged in place by the walls ; any slight play can be taken up by a small wood wedge at one end. It is advisable, however, to secure at least some of the trestle feet to the floor, if this is permissible, either with long panel pins, driven in at an angle, or with metal brackets and small screws. When the baseboard cannot be made a close fit between walls some bracing or staying is necessary to check the kind of movement shown in Fig. 4. The simplest way, and the most economical in the use of material, is to secure some of the trestles to the wall with Rawlplugs and iron brackets as shown in Fig. 5. This avoids the need for additional timber, but there are cases where the walls must not be defaced, even by Rawlplugs. The simplest alternative is shown in

Fig. 6. Wooden stays are fixed with screws from a point near the foot of the trestle to the under-baseboard structure. Such diagonal stays need not be made from the regular 2 in. by 1 in. battening. Like the diagonal members of the trestles, already mentioned, they can be made of almost any odds and ends of timber, and such defects as mild shakes are not usually of much account. It should not be necessary to fit braces to every trestle ; every second or third should provide enough rigidity, but others can be added later if it is found necessary. It may be added that if no timber should be available

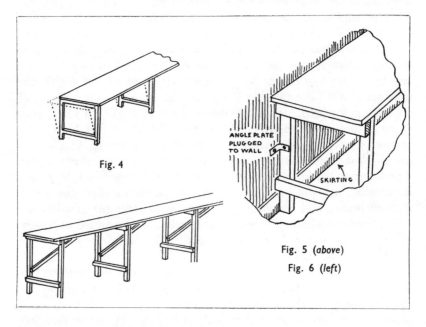

ANGLE PLATE
PLUGGED
TO WALL

SKIRTING

Fig. 4

Fig. 5 (*above*)

Fig. 6 (*left*)

for this purpose but flat strip iron is, there is no objection to the use of the latter, provided, of course, that it is sufficiently strong not to whip under compression.

Tubular metal construction, of the kind used extensively for factory and laboratory benches, has not been investigated as far as the writer knows, except by some of the model railway clubs in the United States for large club layouts. If the necessary materials can be obtained it would make a very substantial and satisfactory foundation for a model railway, and the cost might prove to be little, if at all, higher than that of timber.

The reader should have no difficulty in obtaining suitable

material. Ordinary deal is entirely satisfactory, but it should be noted that all deals are not alike and that considerable variations in quality are to be found. Sappy, unseasoned stuff should be avoided as far as possible and an effort should be made to pick out material which has a reasonably straight grain. Wood in which the grain twists and runs off at an angle is almost sure to twist and warp in a few months. If they cannot be avoided entirely, such pieces should be used in positions where distortion is not likely to produce serious consequences. Wood which has large knots should also be used with care. A knot means a weak place; demonstrated by the fact that a knot will sometimes shrink until it falls out, leaving a hole. Hence, if you have to use a piece of battening, disfigured by a large knot, in a position where it will be under load it is advisable to screw another piece of wood (or a metal plate) across the weak point with several wood screws on each side. Do not accept meekly whatever the timber merchant chooses to give you; he may take the opportunity to unload some of the rubbish—and he will not charge any less for it. Don't be aggressive with him and don't pretend to more knowledge than you actually possess, but just show an intelligent interest in what you are getting. It is often possible to avoid knots, or at least to avoid them in places where it matters, by a little intelligent foresight in marking out before cutting.

During the years after the war, a certain amount of deal was offered for sale which was, to say the least of it, not free from disease. All timber should be examined for possible symptoms before use. A few worm holes are unlikely to be serious and should be treated with Rentokil Timber Fluid, made by Rentokil Ltd., 16, Dover Street, London, W.1, and obtainable from chemists and hardware stores, but evidence of dry rot is quite another matter. Any wood which is affected by this disease should be removed from the house *at once* and burnt as soon as possible. It is very unlikely that the reader will be offered timber so affected, but if in doubt he should obtain the advice of someone who knows how to recognise the symptoms. The commonest test is to insert the blade of a pocket knife into the wood ; if it offers less than the normal resistance, having regard to the type of wood and its natural hardness, and if it fails to grip the blade, so that a slight effort is required to release it, dry rot is certainly present and expert advice should be sought.

That the danger is real is demonstrated by the fact that several years ago the writer bought two boards from a reputable source which were found to contain dry rot in an advanced state and had to be destroyed.

BASEBOARDS

We may assume that the reader has arrived at the stage where a structure of 2 in. by 1 in. battening, looking something like Fig. 1, has been erected. The longitudinal members will be, normally, about 10 in. to 12 in. apart, and the supporting trestles may stand at intervals of about 3 ft. 6 in. to 4 ft. It will be noted from the illustrations that the longitudinal members are placed in the upright position to secure greater resistance to downward pressure. We must

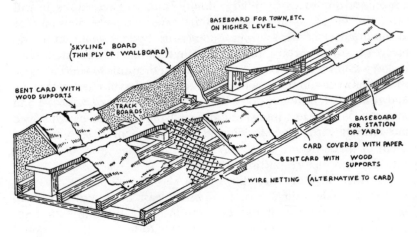

Fig. 7

now consider what form the actual baseboard of the railway is to assume. The old method was to cover the substructure all over with planks or with some form of medium-hard wallboard, such as Ensonite. But as mentioned in the introductory chapter the drawback to this method is that it is apt to result in a rather depressingly flat arrangement, in which hills or differences of level rise with rather unnatural abruptness from the uncompromising " datum " level provided by the baseboard. It may be added that at present-day prices it will be quite an expensive business to form the whole of the baseboard for a railway of any size in this way, whether wood or wallboard is used, although some will be needed in any case.

The considerations mentioned above are strong arguments in

favour of what is called the " open table top " form of construction, which seems to have had its origin in the United States. Apart from requiring much less expensive material, and encouraging the use of less valuable ones, such as card and paper, it allows, and in fact demands, greater freedom in the handling and arrangement of scenic effects. The reader is invited to consider Fig. 7, where as much information as possible has been inserted. For station or yard layouts a section of solid table-top, wood, or compressed board, is installed in the traditional manner. This can be seen on the right of the drawing. But for other parts of the system the tracks are laid on narrow strips of wood or wallboard which need be only as wide as the track formation, say 2 in. or 3 in. for a single track in " OO " gauge, and about twice this for double track. These track boards can be nailed or screwed direct to the substructure, if the line runs at minimum baseboard level, or raised on supports made from odd pieces of wood, usually the ends left over from the substructure, if it is at a higher level. Roads are formed in the same way. The open spaces between the track boards can be covered over in several ways, and it is here that we approach the art of miniature landscape and scenery. Ways and means of completing the terrain through which our railroad runs are considered in the next chapter.

CHAPTER TWO

The Landscape Foundation

THE most obvious advantage of the open table-top method (apart from a considerable economy of material) is that it facilitates the making of such features as hollows, river valleys, and harbours, which must be below the normal baseboard level. With an all-over baseboard these can be formed only by sawing out chunks of it, and the prospect of this often appears so intimidating that the builder is effectively discouraged from making the attempt. In most other respects the method can be much the same whether an open or a closed table-top is used.

The materials employed for the foundations of the terrain can be determined to a considerable extent by what may happen to be available, and by the inclinations of the builder. Briefly stated, the normal procedure is to build up a rough, and quite irregular, foundation on which some form of plaster or modelling clay can be spread to represent the top soil, exposed rock, etc. The foundation may consist of card and paper, and odd pieces of pressed board and ply fixed with pins and glue over a rough framework of odd pieces of wood, assembled with screws and nails on the baseboard or substructure. The wood framework may be made of the ends left over from the construction of the baseboards, from orange boxes and packing cases broken up for the purpose, or from almost any other material which may be available. Upon this framework many workers prefer to mould wire netting, in preference to card, fixing it with panel or veneer pins, driven only part of the way in and bent over to form a hook by which the netting is secured. This is illustrated in Fig. 8, and in the photograph on page 13. A covering of brown paper, packing paper, or sacking, is laid on the netting with a liberal application of glue or glue size.

A material is now obtainable known as expanded duralumin, which resembles wire netting in appearance but is pressed and expanded by a factory process from sheet metal. It is used for many commercial purposes, such as the safety guards on gas fires, and its ornamental qualities are employed with considerable ingenuity in shop window display fittings. The mesh is of a diamond form, and for the purpose under consideration it is preferable to ordinary wire netting. It can be moulded in the hands to practically any shape, and is sufficiently strong to be used practically without support, except, perhaps, at a few widely spaced strategic points. The writer knows of at least one large model railway upon which it is used exclusively as a scenic foundation. If the reader has difficulty in obtaining it he might apply to Messrs. Buck & Ryan Ltd., 310, Euston Road, London, N.W.1, as this firm is known to carry stocks.

In Fig. 7 several ways of building up the terrain between the track boards are illustrated. We have sections of bent and crumpled card laid on rough wood supports and nailed to the substructure and to the edges of the track boards. It will be noticed that the embankment in the lower part of the drawing on the left can be made to dip to form a hollow or valley, there being no continuous table-top to get in the way. Crumpled brown paper is also shown, laid with glue or gum on the card foundation, but this may not always be required if a plaster or modelling clay is used. Hereafter the term " earth-mix " will be used as a general name to cover all such materials when used for this purpose.

For the next stage a choice between two methods is open to us, but although it is convenient here to speak of a choice of methods it should be understood that in practice they can be used together freely, and as convenience may indicate ; there is nothing mutually exclusive about them. We can either apply an earth-mix over the foundation or we can work direct, with paints, sand, sawdust, and other materials, on a base of crumpled paper. The writer usually favours the earth-mix method and will describe it later ; we may deal first with the paper base method. Unless the card or wire netting foundation is reasonably rigid it is advisable to use two layers of paper. Newspaper can be used, at least for the underlayer, but brown paper, or packing paper, provides a more convenient colour to work on. Usually the paper should be applied in pieces not more than about 1 ft. square. They should be well crumpled between the hands and spread out on a pile of old newspapers while glue or gum is brushed on rather thickly. They are then laid in place on the foundation. The writer uses ordinary office gum for this purpose because it is easily and quickly applied and always ready for use. He keeps a large bottle (about quart size) on hand, and decants a quantity into a wide-mouthed jar for immediate use. Use a fairly large soft brush. One about 1 in. to 1½ in. wide is convenient. For the top layer it is better for the edges of the paper to be torn rather than cut with scissors, for an irregular and ragged edge will not call attention to itself after the scenic work has been completed as a hard straight one might. When two layers of paper, with plenty of glue or gum between, have been laid on even a comparatively flimsy foundation it is surprising how rigid and serviceable it becomes. Fig. 7 also shows the use of wire netting, or expanded duralumin, as an alternative to card.

If the supports for the framework must be fixed to an all-over baseboard the use of small iron angle bracket, or blocks of 2 in. by 2 in. wood, as shown in the small diagram at the foot of Fig. 8 is recommended. This method is equally applicable whether the framework is to be built up with card or wire netting. It is usually easier, and more satisfactory, to fix the supports direct to the 2 in. by 1 in. members of the substructure, although with this method it may sometimes be necessary to add a short crossmember to the substructure in order to provide a support between the main longitudinal members.

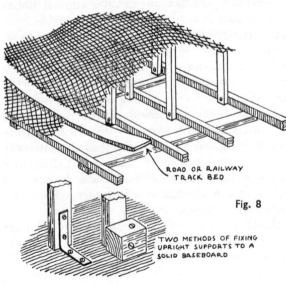

ROAD OR RAILWAY TRACK BED

Fig. 8

TWO METHODS OF FIXING UPRIGHT SUPPORTS TO A SOLID BASEBOARD

In America the most popular form of wire netting for scenic modelling purposes appears to be the fine metal gauze which is used extensively for door and window screens. Our climate does nor oblige us to use such screens and this material would probably be difficult to obtain here, but the ordinary galvanised wire

Common wire netting in use as the foundation of a cliff face.

chicken netting, with a mesh of about ½ in. or a little more, is quite suitable. The expanded duralumin, mentioned above, is preferable however.

As an alternative to paper the framework can be covered with sacking material, or hessian from which the dressing has been removed by soaking in water. It should be treated with glue, glue size, or gum, the most suitable adhesive in this case being, perhaps, glue size. When such materials are used over a card foundation, apply glue or size to the foundation first, lay the material in position, and immediately apply another coat on top of the material so that it is well impregnated. When using wire netting the material should be laid in position and a good coat of the adhesive applied and worked into the fibres, so that some of it goes through and adheres to the metal support. It is advisable to use a large brush ; an old distemper brush is very suitable if one happens to be available. With a smaller brush the job will be rather slow and laborious because the material will absorb the adhesive so rapidly that it will be necessary to recharge the brush every few moments.

At this stage the builder should, as far as possible, have a broad idea in his mind of " the lie of the land " and the nature of the country he is modelling : arable, rolling downs, moorland, mountains. By the lie of the land I refer more particularly to the general direction in which water would be expected to run. If a river is included everything adjoining will naturally be more or less conditioned by it, since the land will necessarily fall in that direction. A river is a most valuable scenic feature as it provides a strong focus of interest and makes the planning of a model landscape very much easier. The river provides a kind of backbone, from which everything else can radiate. It should not be forgotten that rivers have

A comprehensive photograph which illustrates a number of useful details. On the left is the foundation for a winding railway cutting in process of erection. Shaped formers of pulp board, longitudinal wood supports (from an orange box), and cardboard will be noticed. Towards the centre there is a road, cut from thick card, which runs above the river and gradually descends to the level of the railway track on the left. On the right there is more hillside work and we see a foundation composed of strips of wood and card bridging the gap between the higher and lower level baseboards.

small streams feeding them, and these also can be used to good purpose. The best inspiration for such work is observation of the habits and characteristics of an actual stretch of country ; a study of large scale contour maps is helpful.

EARTH-MIXES

We may now consider some of the plastic modelling materials which we have called earth-mixes. Many materials have been used by different workers to represent earth and rock and perhaps one of the earliest of which any record exists is papier mache. The writer's objection to this is that from all published accounts it appears to take an inordinately long time to dry out sufficiently for further work to be undertaken, and protracted delays, running to more than a week by some accounts, are thoroughly bad for artistic inspiration. Whatever material is used should set hard overnight so that work can be resumed next day.

Ordinary decorator's plaster is cheap and convenient, but not very satisfactory. It is likely to develop cracks after a time and may crumble if the base is not very rigid. A mixture described by George Allen in the *Model Railroader* sounds good, and merits a trial if the materials can be obtained. It consists of six parts of shredded asbestos to one part of water glass (sodium silicate). The instructions given are to dampen the asbestos thoroughly before mixing with the water glass, and then to add water slowly until a suitable consistency is obtained. Mr. Allen claims that it will not crack or shrink.

Another American formula, used by Richard Houghton, consists of three or four parts of whiting or gypsum to one part of Casco glue. These ingredients are mixed to a useful consistency with water. It seems possible that some of the scumble finishes supplied for decorative wall treatment might provide a useful earth-mix.

The writer's particular fancy is Alabastine Filler mixed with sawdust. This provides a very convenient modelling clay of a slightly rough and gritty texture ; it takes oil or water colour well and dries out in a day or less according to the thickness of the work. The instructions printed on the carton specify that two and a half parts by bulk of the Alabastine Filler should be mixed to a paste with one part water. This proportion of two and a half parts of solid to one of water should be adhered to when mixing although it may occasionally be necessary to add a few drops more water before use, or during use, but the proportions of Alabastine to sawdust can be varied within considerable limits provided the ratio of solids to liquid is maintained. Thus we can use two parts Alabastine and half a part of sawdust or one and half parts Alabastine and one part sawdust. The writer now uses the last-mentioned proportions almost exclusively. A cup can be used to measure the constituents ; it will not need any elaborate cleaning afterwards and can be returned to domestic use after being rinsed. The materials can be put in a pudding basin or old saucepan, and should be thoroughly mixed with a stick or a spoon. The mixture made as described would be almost dead white, which is not a very convenient colour upon which to work. Any patches, however small, which may be missed when painting will show up rather unpleasantly, and poster colours, being rather thin, are likely to lack body if laid on white. For these reasons the writer adds a small quantity of powder colour, brown or red, of the kind sold by oil and colour merchants. No attempt has

Fig. 9

TIPPED ROCK STRATA, FORMED BY DRAWING LINES ACROSS THE WET PLASTIC MATERIAL. NOTE PLANTS GROWING ON LEDGES AND AT BASE OF CLIFF

been made to measure the quantity because the exact depth of tone is quite unimportant, provided the dead white is killed. A teaspoonful to about a pint of the mixture should be sufficient. The mixture will dry considerably lighter than it appears while wet. It can be laid on with an old knife or with a small trowel. The crevices of rock strata can be suggested by drawing the point of a screwdriver, or some similar tool, across the surface. The earth-mix will be found easier to manage if the tools used for laying and moulding it are dipped in water from time to time. This prevents the mix adhering to them and the worker should keep a bowl of water within reach for the purpose. Experience will soon suggest certain differences in the method of handling for different kinds of ground. The earth-mix should be smoothed off for grassland and downs, but left rough, with the marks of the knife or trowel visible, for broken ground and rock. Fig. 9 offers some suggestions as to how a cliff face, with sloping and unequally weathered strata, may be worked up. Small rocks and pebbles can be worked in and the earth-mix built up round them. The average thickness need not exceed ⅛ in. and may be less ; in fact, on suitable surfaces the mix can be treated more as a thick coat of paint. It is sometimes necessary, however, to lay it on quite thickly, and if a thickness of more than about ⅜ in. is required it is better to apply two coats, the first being allowed to dry before the second is laid on. In such cases one can economise earth-mix by inserting odd scraps of wood and covering them over.

This Alabastine earth-mix will stick securely to any surface which is sufficiently rigid to provide a firm bed for it : paper, hardened with glue, card, wood, or sacking. It cannot, of course, be applied to wire netting without some intermediate support, unless the mesh is very fine.

As far as the writer has been able to discover, this mixture will not crack even if some clumsy individual should lean on the scenery and distort it out of shape. This is probably due, at least in part, to the presence of the sawdust, which appears to give the Alabastine flexibility without impairing its cohesion. After several years' experience it has never been known to break away from any surface.

The writer occasionally makes use of Pyruma as an earth-mix. It has the advantage of being ready for immediate use, so that no time is wasted in preparation. It is, therefore, useful for filling up odd corners for which it is not worth while to make up a supply of the Alabastine mix. Possibly its colour and texture may render it particularly suitable for the representation of some kinds of rock, and the modeller is recommended to keep a tin in stock even if it is only required occasionally. If it is found to have become hard in the tin, it can be " brought back " by working in a little water. The objection has been expressed that Pyruma remains liable to be affected by damp in the atmosphere after it has hardened. This is not a valid objection to its use because if the room in which the model work is installed is so damp as to produce any effect on Pyruma the fact will certainly become evi-

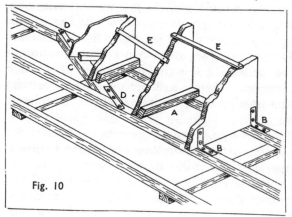

Fig. 10

dent in other and more alarming ways. Such a room would, in fact, be quite unfit to house a model railway or anything else of any importance, and it would be evident that some serious structural trouble was present in the building.

There seems to be no reason why ordinary Keen's cement should not be quite satisfactory as an earth-mix, but the writer has had no experience of it for this purpose. It can be mixed quickly and without the necessity of measuring quantities. It is only necessary to pour some out of the packet into a bowl and to stir in water with a stick until it reaches the right consistency. It hardens very quickly and for this reason should be useful for work which must be built up to a considerable depth.

When steep embankments, and what we may loosely define as mountain masses, are to be produced, the form of framework suggested in Fig. 10 and the photographs on page 27 is most suitable. The shaped upright sections (usually referred to, although rather inaccurately, as contours) can be cut with a keyhole saw from any odd pieces of wood or compressed board. A soft board is to be preferred as the cutting is a rather exhausting business in harder material. They can be shaped quite roughly and the waste piece left over from one will usually provide another with little or no modification. In Fig. 10 such " contours " are shown in association with the open table-top form of construction, but they could, of course, be erected on a solid baseboard. They can be fixed in place with strips of wood and nails or screws as at A, or with iron angle brackets from almost any ironmonger or hardware store as at B. It may be pointed out here that when the softest kind of pulp board is used it may sometimes be advisable to put washers under the heads of any screws used for fixing purposes as a safeguard against the possibility of the spongy material pulling away from the screw. Similarly, for the form of fixing shown at B in Fig. 10 it would be safer to use nuts and bolts with a fairly large washer on the side opposite to the iron bracket. Whether such precautions are necessary depends, of course, on whether the material is likely to be subjected to any serious strain or not.

When diagonally placed crossmembers are required, as shown at C, the flat, drilled, iron-plates D from Woolworth's or a hardware store, are usually the most convenient means of securing them.

If the sections or " contours " are not more than six or eight inches apart, a rough cardboard covering, or wire netting, can be nailed to them without any additional support. If they are more widely spaced they should be joined first with occasional wood slats, as at EE, for greater stability.

TRACK BOARDS

We may conclude this chapter with some notes on the track boards upon which the railway itself is to be laid, and their relationship to the scenic work. They can be made of planking or match-boarding, or some form of semi-hard wallboard. By " semi-hard " I refer to those varieties which offer about the same amount of resistance as the softer kind of white deal when a nail or a screw is driven into them. The softer kinds of board (often referred to as pulpboard) are not recommended where track is to be laid as they do not provide a firm hold for pins or nails, and trouble may occur due to the track springing up in some places. There is also the risk that if some of the pins are driven in with more force than others,

This photograph shows track boards cut from Ensonite and fixed with panel pins to the timber substructure. Notice that in the foreground the boards have been cut with a keyhole saw to give the shape for the banks of a river and that part of the " bed," cut from a cheaper and thinner material, is in position at the lower level provided by the trans-verse members of the substructure. It will be seen that the junction between two sections of baseboard occurs on the right of the photograph. These sections could be separated, if necessary, by the removal of three long screws from underneath.

the rather spongy surface may compress locally under the sleepers with results which are equally inimical to good running. If the track is built up in sections on a solid road-bed, of the type supplied by ERG (Bournemouth) Ltd., this objection should not apply as the track already has a solid foundation under it. Plywood can be used for the track boards but is not recommended on account of the difficulty of inducing pins and small nails to penetrate the successive layers of glue without bending. Plywood, if used, requires to be supported at more frequent intervals than most other materials because, due to the extreme hardness imparted to it by the glue layers, it will be found to vibrate in a maddening manner when an attempt is made to drive in a nail about midway between supports.

If the positions of the tracks can be determined exactly in advance of laying, the track boards need be no more than formation width, and can, if desired, be chamfered at the edges to represent the banking up of the ballast and the drainage ditches. That is no doubt the ideal way, but it often happens that the constructor does not wish to determine the exact formation of the tracks until he comes to the actual laying, and he may have the possibility of future alterations and realignments in mind. In such cases a practical compromise is indicated, and we may cut our track boards perhaps 6 in. to 1 ft. wide to allow some margin for possible changes of plan. This is the method usually employed by the writer. We may suppose that these wide track boards will in most cases be partly covered with scenic work, which can always be modified if the need should arise later.

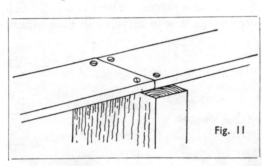

Fig. 11

The track boards are supported at suitable intervals (governed by the strength and thickness of the material) on wood blocks which are screwed to the substructure, and for rising gradients these supports are graduated in height. This is illustrated in Fig. 7. Where the ends of two track boards meet they should be attached with nails or screws to a support as shown in Fig. 11. It is preferable to use screws because then any irregularity in the level caused, perhaps, by a slight difference in the thickness of the boards, can be adjusted without difficulty by releasing the screws holding one of them and inserting thin card or wood packing underneath. This applies with additional emphasis to gradients.

For station and yard layouts, and usually for model towns and villages, we lay a section of baseboard on the substructure in the traditional manner. Usually it can be made of the same material as the track boards, but there is no objection to the soft pulp boards for the sites of towns and villages where no tracks are to be laid. The writer lays such boards with 1 in. panel pins. Most wallboards require to be fixed at only a few points, but with wood a little more care is necessary to guard against possible warping. If the baseboard is to occupy an elevated position above the substructure, it is attached to wood supports as shown in the top right hand corner of Fig. 7.

If it should be necessary to lay railway tracks on soft pulpboard, from motives of economy or on account of shortage of material, the writer suggests that the floating track system, used by Mr. Fleetwood Shawe, should be tried. Mr. Shawe lays his track on felt or sheet rubber, and the fixing pins are left projecting 1/32 in. above the sleepers. Thus the rails are free to depress under the weight of the trains. It is reasonable to expect that most readers will at first feel strongly prejudiced against this system, but the writer can only say that on Mr. Shawe's layout it seems to give better and more reliable running than a rigidly fixed track. It should be added that Mr. Shawe is careful to ensure that every piece of rail is straight before it is laid and that all fishplate joints are made with more than ordinary care to ensure that the rails shall be level and in line.

CHAPTER THREE

Scenic Treatment of the Ground

IT was indicated in the last chapter that there was more than one method of working up the ground to represent grass, earth, rock, and other surfaces, and that the application of an earth-mix may not be considered essential where a surface of crumpled paper of a brownish colour and rather rough texture has been provided. The writer has occasionally worked direct with paints, sand, and other materials, on a surface of this kind. It is also possible to work direct on surfaces such as sacking and hessian, and this method may commend itself if it is necessary to produce finished results in a hurry, as may happen when large models are being prepared for display and exhibition purposes. The result can be entirely satisfactory in the case of work which is to be viewed by spectators who are separated from the model by a barrier rail, and under lighting arrangements which can be controlled by the exhibitor, but for the more intimate conditions of the home model railway the use of an earth-mix, as described in the last chapter, is preferable and may involve no more work in the long run. Both methods can be used on the same layout and in this way the modeller can determine for himself which he prefers. At the worst the resulting difference in tone and texture, due to the use of two methods, will only tend to suggest differences in the nature of the soil, by no means an uncommon phenomenon in nature. Even that will tend to become less noticeable when the colours have become slightly faded by the action of light and dust. And it is as well to remember that nothing is final or irrevocable in this form of modelling : if the result is not considered entirely satisfactory after a time one can always try a different kind of paint—over the first attempt—or a different grass mixture or something else, and if the result still does not seem satisfactory one can cover the whole with a fresh layer of earth-mix and start again. The modeller need not be afraid to experiment for it is practically impossible to make a mistake which cannot be repaired. It should be remembered, however, that it is difficult to lay poster colours on a dark toned surface and that if this should be necessary it is advisable to use something with better covering power, such as oils or distemper.

We may now list the materials which in the writer's experience are most useful in working up the ground, and then consider their application. The principal ones are:

Paints: Poster colours and flat oils. Distempers and tempera colours can also be used.

Sand: Both the coarse red and the much finer silver kinds are required and are used for different purposes.

Sawdust: The sawdust from almost any wood is suitable if reasonably fine. If mixed with splinters and small shavings it is advisable to sift it.

Sawdust dyed green to represent grass, etc.

Adhesives: Casco glue and ordinary office gum are the most used. Durofix and Bostik D (the white kind) may also be found useful.

Materials used to represent trees and bushes will be considered separately.

The reader should not be content to accept any ready-made list of materials however ; he should be constantly looking out for materials which can be pressed into service. Chicken grit and powdered cork, coloured chalks and charcoal, may all have their uses. Maw seed, obtainable from cornchandlers at about three shillings a pound, appears to be an almost ideal grey ballast for model railways in " OO " and " O " gauges. It should be useful also for granite or slate scree on hillsides. Small stones and gravel are also useful.

Of the above-mentioned properties green sawdust calls for some explanation. It is sprinkled on an adhesive to represent grass, leaves, and undergrowth. In earlier editions of this book I described the preparation of green sawdust with the domestic packet dyes which were then available. I felt obliged to add a warning that sawdust so prepared had to be used with discretion because the colour was liable to become degraded if the material was applied with any adhesive having a water base. This description appears to include office gum (in other respects a most useful adhesive for scenic work), and tube glues of the Seccotine and Croid type, but not Durofix or Bostik D. The trouble appeared to be due to the dyed sawdust remaining absorbent and " sucking up " the adhesive. I am pleased to say that a dye is now generally on sale which, as far as I can discover, overcomes this difficulty entirely. This is sold under the name Dylon and the shade which is most useful for grass is numbered 23 on the colour card. No doubt other shades could be used for dark tree foliage or for ivy, shade number 26 perhaps. This is excellent news and means that the modeller can now use dyed sawdust more freely than heretofore.

Dissolve the dye solution in an old saucepan, or a tin which can be trusted not to leak, and bring it to the boil. The sawdust is heaped on a square of muslin and the corners brought together and tied with string, or wire, to form a bag within which the sawdust is enclosed. About a foot of the string or wire should be left free to provide a handhold by which the bag can be lowered into the dye bath and subsequently withdrawn from it. The sawdust should be lowered into the gently boiling dye and left there for about fifteen minutes. It should be prodded frequently with a piece of stick, both to keep it below the surface and to ensure that the dye penetrates right through the mass and reaches every part.

Opinions are bound to differ as to the best shade to represent grass, but the following seems to answer well for most purposes:

Dylon (shade No. 23) Chartreuse ...	30 grains
Water	1 pint

Since some readers will not have chemical scales it may be said that 30 grains is perhaps rather more than half a flat teaspoonful. But since in practice more than a pint is wanted—two pints being about the minimum useful bath—measurement does not present a problem as our quantity for two pints is a heaped teaspoon. There is no need to be very exact about it. It should be understood that it is impossible to estimate the final colour either from the appearance of the dye or of the sawdust while wet; it will dry several shades lighter. When the sawdust is removed from the dye bath, it should be held over the vessel for a minute or two while it drains. The bag is then opened and the contents spread out to dry, preferably on a sheet of metal, such as an old tin tray. It should be spread as thinly as possible to allow the air to circulate freely for drying is apt to be a slow process.

It should be put, if possible, in a warm place, above a stove or on a hot water tank.

The dye bath may be kept for use a second time within a few days, but it should be put away somewhere where the children (if any) or the cat quite definitely cannot get at it.

Green flock powder can be obtained in packets from Modelcraft or C.C.W. and should be applied in much the same way as green sawdust.

The working up of the ground surface is a distinctly individual business in which most workers will soon develop their own methods and dodges. The first step, generally speaking, is to tint the ground with appropriate colours for the surfaces to be represented : green for grassland, brown for gravel and exposed earth, and so on. Work very broadly with a large brush, at least an inch wide. In most cases the exact shades are not very important for this is to be regarded as more in the nature of a preliminary tinting than anything else. It helps the worker to sort out his ideas and obtain a broad view of the general effect he is aiming at. With exposed rock on cliffs and outcroppings, however, it is advisable to work a little more carefully at this stage because very little subsequent work may be necessary, beyond the application of a little silver-sand on an adhesive to improve the texture and soften the colours, and a few touches of green paint or green sawdust to represent moss and rock plants. We shall return to this subject later.

For this first treatment, poster colour or Reeves' tempera colour may be used. Note that the word treatment is used, and not the word coat, because the latter would suggest the idea of painting in the decorator's sense, which is something altogether more " all overish," and heavy handed than we want here. On brown paper of the darker kinds, poster colour is less suitable, as it lacks the covering power required by the darker surface and tempera or oil colour should be used. For hessian and sacking also tempera or oil colour is preferable, especially if a large area is to be covered. Distemper can be used, but presents the difficulty that it is impossible to judge the colour while it is wet. This may not be so serious when large areas are to be covered in a rather wholesale manner, but becomes more important when delicate and detailed effects are sought. The disability can be overcome, to some extent, by preparing a set of sample cards of various distempers which can be used as a guide while working.

When the first colour application has had time to dry we can embark on the finishing processes, which vary considerably with the

This and the following six photographs demonstrate successive stages in the building of a section of scenic model railway. Above the sub-structure has been completed, the track boards, which climb to the level of the bridge through a river valley, mounted on wood supports of graduated height, and some of the track laid. The " bed " of the river is in place and the erection of skyline boards, which form the foundation of the background scenery, has just commenced on the extreme left. The rather indeterminate horizontal line, a few inches above the track boards, is the *lower edge* of a skyblue background which is suspended from the wall. It consists of distempered wallpaper and is fixed along the top edge only. The lower edge will be completely concealed by the built-up scenic work in due course.

A cellophane covering has now been laid on the river and the banks cut from soft " Treetex " with a keyhole saw. The skyline boards, made of $\frac{1}{4}$ in. Essex board are in position and sundry formers, or supports, of wood and pulp board, begin to appear above the railway track. Notice the gap in the skyline boards where the river wanders off into the distance through a break in the line of the hills. Below the track a foundation of card is being built to form the slope between the track boards and the river bank.

Odd pieces of card and thin wood are being nailed in place on the formers
to complete the foundation for the steep slope beyond the railway. This
framework will be covered with brown paper, treated with glue, and
then with an earth-mix.

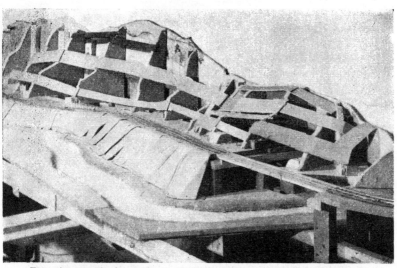

This photograph shows the work at the same stage as the last, but the
camera has been shifted to a position more to the right. The bridge,
which carries the railway across the river, is at present represented by
nothing more than a strip of wood which serves as the deck.

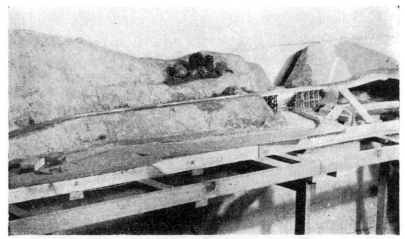

Most of the rough foundation has now been covered with paper and with Alabastine earth-mix, and the actual scenic work is in progress. The bridge has acquired timber trestles, one of which has been painted while the other has not. On the extreme right a small section of the hillside has not yet been covered with the earth-mix. It is distinguished by the darker tone of the brown paper.

This is a close-up view of the bridge, taken at the same stage as the last photograph. We can now see that the trestles were built up separately on bases of $\frac{1}{8}$-in. plywood and just pushed into position under the neck of the bridge. Their height was adjusted as accurately as possible, but no harm would have resulted if they had been a trifle short as they could have been packed up underneath with card. It will be seen on the left that the bases of the trestles are concealed by extending the scenic work to cover them. Stripwood and $\frac{3}{16}$-in. dowel rod was employed in the construction of the trestles and they were assembled with glue and fine pins. The plywood bases were drilled to house the feet of the upright members.

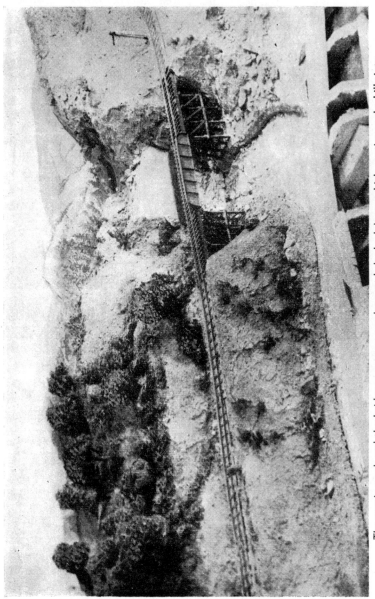

The scenic work and the bridge are now complete, and the backdrop, which continues the hills into the distance, is in position. The lower edge of the skyblue background is no longer seen. Work is still in progress on the bank of the river in the extreme foreground.

kind of surface represented.   It is now that the work, which heretofore may have seemed rather unreal and discouraging, should begin to come to life.

GRASS AND FOLIAGE

For grass and foliage, as has been mentioned already, we have a choice between two methods.   We can spread an adhesive on the surface with a brush and sprinkle green dyed sawdust on it.

The second method is to sprinkle ordinary undyed sawdust over an adhesive and, when dry, to paint it with a rather sloppy yellowish green oil paint.   Almost any kind of oil colour can be used, matt decorators' colour in tins, decorators' colour in tubes, or artists' colours.   The last named are the most costly.   A brilliant and rather deep yellow is wanted and a smaller quantity of almost any medium green.   Such a mixture can be adjusted, by varying the proportions, to give the exact colour required, and will probably produce better results than any paint which can be bought ready mixed.   The trouble with practically all ready mixed green paints is that they are too blue for grass, although some are quite suitable for the darker tones of foliage.   The writer's method is to ladle some of the yellow into the lid of a tin, with a stick which is used for stirring.   Then just enough green is added to give a definite greenish tinge.   It is better to add too little green rather than too much, for it is difficult to realise what a high proportion of yellow there is in the ordinary greens of nature, and we are trying to adjust our colours to the circumstance that model railways are viewed by artificial light more often than otherwise.   Blue is a colour which does not take kindly to half-watt light, and must be employed with caution.   The paint should be used rather thinly and dabbed on (rather than painted on in the normal sense) with an old brush.   If the paint is too thick the result may appear rather opaque and clotted ; it is better to go over the work a second time if necessary.

Trees and hedges (considered later) are treated in the same way with sawdust and paint, but the colour can usually be somewhat darker.   Please note that darker does not mean a higher proportion of blue.   The more or less olive tones of many trees and hedges are better represented by the addition of a little *black*.   A soft brush and thin paint are necessary for it calls for perseverance to make the paint penetrate the foliage sufficiently.   I do not like the method of dipping as the paint then penetrates too much, producing an ' all overish ' effect.

EARTH AND GRAVEL

The writer's method for these is to apply a sprinkling of sand over a brown paint of appropriate tint. Poster colour seems as suitable as oils, and is certainly more convenient since it dries very quickly. The colour of the surface soil varies enormously in different districts, from black through different shades of brown to the yellow of wet clay and the red soil which can be found in some parts of Devonshire. The darker tones should be avoided in any case (except for very local use to provide notes of contrast) as they do not show to advantage under artificial light. One can always break down colours which are too dark by the addition of white. In scenic work it is necessary to be constantly on guard against the difference between outdoor and indoor light, even when the latter is natural daylight entering the room through windows.

Raw umber is a good basic colour for earth and gravel. It can be used alone or mixed with small quantities of other colours such as burnt sienna (red), sepia, or yellow ochre. A little white can be added if it is feared that the colour will be too dark or too intense, and in this connection it should be remembered that by comparison with the greens of nature the browns usually assume a rather soft pastel quality. We have to consider the question of viewpoint, and the effect of distance, when colouring scenery. We naturally tend to look at a model landscape more or less as a whole, and the writer feels that everything should be treated as it would appear at a distance of at least 50 to 100 yd. This is explained by the fact that if you look at 4 mm. scale modelwork at a normal distance of about 3 ft., you are viewing it from the scale equivalent distance of just over 200 ft. It is, of course, true that you may sometimes examine a model at much closer range than 3 ft., but to do so is the exception. The worker is well advised to take this fact into account both in his choice of colours and in assessing the amount of detail which it is worth while to include. Distance exercises a softening effect so that at the extreme limit of vision all colours tend to become grey, and this should serve as a warning against hard, over-brilliant colours, especially in the background ; the parts of the scene which are most distant from the observer.

For bare earth the writer sprinkles a mixture of silver sand and coarse red sand on the brown paint, but for some surfaces, such as certain forms of composition board which have a rough and " sympathetic " surface, the sand treatment may be unnecessary. The paint alone may do all that is wanted. It is unusual, however, to find absolutely bare earth, except on agricultural land where it has recently been turned over.   For most purposes the effect will be more natural if a little green sawdust is applied at the same time as the sand to suggest weeds and grass.   On broken waste ground a few pieces of gravel will also help the effect.   Casco glue is useful in cases like this because, since it dries without shine, there is no need for it to be completely covered ; we can leave bare patches without objectionable results.

Weeds tend to take root in the shadow of stones, so the reader can drop a few grains of the green sawdust as close under some of the pieces of gravel as possible, or he can apply a few touches of green paint with a small brush.

For gravel, as found on field paths, sidewalks, and in gardens and farmyards, ordinary red sand can be used alone or with a very little green sawdust to represent weeds which are breaking through. The basic colour should be a light yellowish brown, lighter and more yellow than would be used for earth.   For a cinder track some of the materials sold as " OO " gauge ballast, which appear to contain a proportion of granite chips, should be suitable.   Another method is to use coarse sand, as for a gravel path, and to paint it over with a matt dark grey paint.   Powdered charcoal might also be useful for this purpose.

ROCKS AND CLIFFS

For the railway modeller cliffs have a special importance, because, due to the limitations of space which usually hamper the full realisation of the worker's ideas, it is sometimes necessary to secure a sharp rise in the level of the ground within a confined space.   The introduction of a cliff may be the only practicable device when high and low level tracks are required to run on the same baseboard.   When two tracks—which in imagination are supposed to be miles apart—have to pursue parallel courses and are in reality only a matter of feet apart, they can be made to appear separate and distinct by the interposition of cliffs or " mountains " which conceal one of them from view.   This is in some ways preferable to the device of a tunnel, which usually creates difficulties in the matter of track maintenance.   There is also the scenic attraction of really wild and mountainous country, insufficiently realised by railway modellers in this country, and the spectacular opportunities it offers for bold scenic features such as viaducts and mountain torrents.

In building up the framework for a cliff, or for a rocky slope, it is advisable to break up and diversify the surface by providing ledges which are near enough level for vegetation to take root and for trees to grow, and where boulders which have become detached from the face higher up can come to rest.   All this tends to increase the illusion of height and depth.   With a suitable earth-mix such plastic modelling is easily built up.   To economise the plastic material, and facilitate the formation of an irregular surface, odd scraps of wood, or composition board, can be placed on the foundation and covered in with the earth-mix as suggested at *x* in Fig. 12.

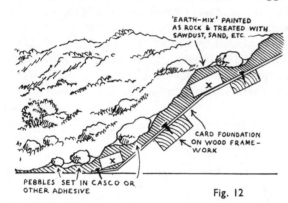

'EARTH-MIX' PAINTED
AS ROCK & TREATED WITH
SAWDUST, SAND, ETC.

CARD FOUNDATION
ON WOOD FRAME-
WORK

PEBBLES SET IN CASCO OR
OTHER ADHESIVE

Fig. 12

It will be seen that these blocks, or fillers, form the foundation for ledges as proposed above. When paper is used as the foundation it will be found that it does not lend itself quite so readily to this treatment, but the card foundation can be bent to form ledges while being nailed down to the wood framework, as in Figure 13, and roughly shaped wedges of paper can be inserted under the paper covering as shown in the same diagram.

The correct colouring of rock surfaces is obviously important, and it is worth while to go to some trouble to obtain the right effect. The delicate tones of poster colours seem to the writer more appropriate than the harder and more opaque ones of oils, and those unused to the handling of a brush for such purposes will probably find the former easier to manage.   It is a matter of opinion, however, and every worker will discover in time which medium fits in best with his own outlook and aptitudes.   One very able worker in the United States has stated that he mixes oil and water colours on the same surface, and presumably applies the one while the other is still wet.   It should be possible to obtain some extremely interesting mottled effects in this way, since water and oil colours will not mix, but this is obviously a technique in which much experience and a close acquaintance with rock formation are essential.

A convincing result depends largely on the judicious blending of colours on the surface. A basic colour can be applied and, preferably while it is still wet, small quantities of other colours, or the same one with additions of other colours such as green, black, grey, white or yellow, can be brushed on locally and allowed to blend at the edges.   These local applications of colour should usually be what artists call glazes, meaning that they are thinned sufficiently to allow the basic colour to show through.   The intention usually is to obtain slight changes of tone and tint, rather than a definite change of colour.   If the reader examines almost any rock surface from a distance of 100 yd. or more, he will form the impression that it is a subtle and delicate patchwork of related, but not identical tones.   This may be attributed to a number of causes : the differing angles which parts of the broken surface present to the atmosphere, causing unequal weathering, the presence of minerals, unevenly distributed, slight differences in the composition of the rock, and the presence of water courses running down over the rock or eroding from fissures. The colours of rock (like most other colours in nature) vary so much with local conditions of lighting, soil, and atmosphere, that the modeller can allow himself a considerable margin of latitude in the actual colours he

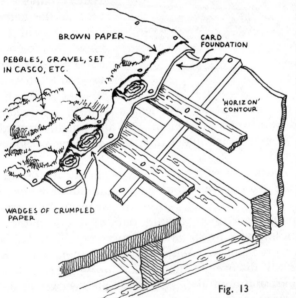

BROWN PAPER

CARD
FOUNDATION

PEBBLES, GRAVEL, SET
IN CASCO, ETC.

'HORIZON'
CONTOUR

WADGES OF CRUMPLED
PAPER

Fig. 13

uses, and it is safe to say that any two landscape artists if asked to paint a scene which includes rock formations from the same viewpoint and under similar lighting conditions would not employ exactly the same mixture of pigments. Bearing this in mind, it is suggested that the following colours may be used to represent the.

common sandstone and limestone of the British Isles as well as any:

| Burnt sienna ... | (red) | Raw umber | ... | (brown) |
| Burnt umber ... | (dark brown) | Yellow ochre |

These can be used in various combinations and should usually be softened slightly by the addition of a little white, or white and black. Perhaps the best combination for sandstone may be produced by using yellow ochre, and adding some burnt sienna, a trace of raw umber, and a little white. The reader should endeavour to check these colours by making use of every opportunity to study actual rock formations, paying particular attention to the general impression produced at a distance of a hundred yards or so.

Fissures and crevices can be formed in the earth-mix, before it hardens, with the blade of a knife or the tang of a file, and it should be remembered that mosses will often take root in such sheltered places, especially if water emerges therefrom. Water issuing from fissures forms runlets which may be laden with green slime which can be represented by lines of green paint pursuing a downward course and tending to follow the hollow and concave parts of the surface. The rock can be made to appear wet by the local application of a gloss varnish, and for this purpose ordinary shellac varnish is as good as anything.

There are, broadly speaking, four groups of rocks which predominate in the British Isles. These are sandstone, limestone, granite and chalk. The reader should use one of these as a basis for his scenic work, having regard to the particular counties he has in mind. Outcroppings of other rocks, especially where tipped strata come to the surface, are quite common, and it is not necessary to assume that the rock in a particular locality is of uniform composition throughout. For aesthetic reasons it is obviously better to assume that the rock is more or less mixed ; the effect of a mixture of colours will be more pleasing and more interesting.

Almost always a number of boulders, of varying sizes, will be found at the foot of a cliff or steep slope, unless somebody has cleared them away for a road or some other purpose. They are, of course, pieces which have become detached and rolled down, and can be represented by large gravel and small stones such as can be picked up in any garden. It is desirable that most of those selected for use should be a reasonably close match to the general colour which has been decided upon for the cliff, although a few odd ones will not be out of place. They should be rinsed under a tap, to remove any soil which may adhere to them, and allowed to dry. For readers who have few opportunities for examining actual rock formations, the best way may be to collect a supply of stones and gravel, and endeavour to mix the paints for the cliff or slope to match their predominant colour as nearly as possible. In making such colour mixtures do not forget that white is likely to be a necessary ingredient.

Stones and gravel should be used liberally at the foot of a cliff or slope, and on any ledges which are large enough to hold them. They can be set in the earth-mix itself, but the writer usually prefers to set them in a bed of thick Casco glue. A little art and imagination is required to produce the best effect ; where there is a depression in the surface of a slope, for example, it is probable that it will have served as a natural highway for falling stones and we may find quite a little moraine where the slope ends or becomes less steep. The spaces between the stones should be covered, before the adhesive sets, with sand and green sawdust, and planted with bushes and patches of scrub as described in a later chapter. The photograph on the opposite page shows a slope made by the writer by the methods outlined here. In selecting stones it is advisable to preserve a sense of scale : a stone about an inch in diameter becomes a boulder more than 6 ft. high in 4 mm. scale. Smooth pebbles which are almost egg-shaped and regular in form, should not be used, because they have no equivalent on a larger scale.

The writer's method of finishing sandstone and limestone, after applying the colour, is to sprinkle fine silver sand on gum or Casco. Casco is preferred, but the gum is quite satisfactory if it is well covered. Patches of green sawdust are worked in at the same time, and the surplus material is brushed off when the adhesive is thoroughly dry. A few remarks may be advisable as to the method of sprinkling sand, sawdust, and similar substances. The writer simply takes a " pinch " between finger and thumb, holds it about a foot above the surface, and allows it to escape slowly with a swinging movement of the arm to distribute it as evenly as possible. The reader could, if he preferred, use a small sieve of some sort with a suitably fine mesh.

For rocks of the granite and slate type it is better to omit the silver-sand treatment, for these have a harder and sometimes a glazed surface which is quite different to that of softer and more porous rocks. For both, the basic colour is a dark grey. For granite, patches or glazes of reddish pink and green should be worked in. Slate also sometimes exhibits a reddish or greenish tinge. Chalk is rather obvious : white with a very small admixture of black to soften and provide tone, and green for the moss which usually manages to appear on parts of the surface. Only comparatively small areas should be quite white ; the greater part should be tinted with greys and greens. Where the angle is not too steep it is usual to find stunted grass or weeds except on a newly exposed quarry face. This effect can be obtained with a little

Close-up view of a rocky hillside, constructed with sand, gravel from the garden (for the boulders), rubberised horsehair, sawdust, and similar properties, on a ground of Alabastine earth-mix. Part of the trestle bridge in the preceding illustrations appears in the top left-hand corner.

green paint, stippled on with an almost dry brush, or with dyed sawdust. In the latter case it is not necessary to cover large areas of the cliff face with the adhesive ; it should be applied here and there with a small brush and the green sawdust sprinkled quite liberally. The surplus which does not adhere will fall to the base of the cliff and can be brushed away later. The characteristic effect at the top of chalk quarry faces should be noted. Usually grass grows right up to the edge, then the soil appears as a brown or reddish line with an even thickness of perhaps a couple of feet, and then the chalk begins.

When representing chalk on a foundation of brown paper, which is rather lacking in texture by comparison with an earth-mix such as Alabastine and sawdust, the writer has remedied the deficiency by applying a layer of silver-sand on gum *before* painting. It will not matter if the sand should show through the paint in places ; it will, in fact, produce a more interesting and diversified effect.

A nice touch when modelling cliffs and cuttings is to introduce strata of another rock of contrasting colour. This can be represented quite easily by a broken and not too irregular brush line which can be allowed to loose itself in places and to reappear, at the same level, farther along the cliff. Or such strata can be tipped at a slight angle and disappear finally into the ground.

In view of what has been said concerning cliffs and slopes, there is little which need be added about railway cuttings, except that we have to distinguish between the kind cut, or blasted, through solid rock, where the walls may be almost vertical, and earth cuttings where the angle is unlikely to exceed about forty degrees. The latter are usually more or less grass grown, unless quite newly excavated. The foundations can take any of the forms which have been described in the foregoing pages : crumpled brown paper, sacking, or an earth-mix.

It has probably occurred to the reader that an alternative method of producing mountainous country would be to use a number of much larger stones than we have so far considered and to fill the spaces between them with an earth-mix, which would serve, also as a cement to bind them together. The process would be rather like building up a stone wall with mortar. Some workers have obtained excellent results by this method. Generally speaking, the earth-mix would not be built up to the level of the rocks, but would be recessed to form gullies which could be treated as soil, and finished with grass and scrub. In appropriate places such gullies could be filled with gravel, of the same kind as the large rocks, laid on a bed of adhesive to represent moraine. This method has the disadvantage of being rather inflexible, and it would be difficult to mix it satisfactorily with scenic work of the kind described in this chapter. The considerable weight on the baseboard structure would also have to be considered.

PLOUGHED FIELDS

Ploughed fields can be represented by a layer of an earth-mix about ⅛ in. thick. Before the material hardens a stick with a blunt point should be drawn over the surface to form the furrows, which for " OO " gauge should be about 6 mm. apart. A length of wood should be used as a guide to ensure that the furrows are approximately straight and regular. It will probably be found necessary to dip the pointed stick in water frequently to prevent the plastic material from sticking to it, and being dragged away from the surface. When the material has hardened it can be sprinkled with sand or sawdust and painted with a deep brown, such as Vandyke brown, to which a little white and black have been added. This will supply the slight neutral tone which is observable in newly-turned earth. If oil colour is used it should be well thinned for we do not want a hard or opaque effect. If necessary, a second thin coat should be applied.

An alternative method of forming a ploughed field is to stick a piece of corrugated packing paper to the baseboard. The surface is treated with gum and a liberal application of sand or sawdust and painted a rather dark greyish brown. The paint should, of course, have no trace of gloss. The edges of the sheet should be concealed by overlapping the earth-mix, or by planting hedges.

Readers who derive amusement from experimenting might care to try their hands at the representation of standing crops. For " OO " gauge a piece of thick pile carpet, dyed to a suitable golden yellow, might be pursuaded to give a fair representation of a field of wheat and would certainly provide a welcome touch of colour to enliven the more sober tones of the natural surroundings. It might be difficult to find a suitable piece of material for this as it would have to be very light in tone to take a light dye. On the other hand, one might find a carpet of a sufficiently light fawn colour to give a good effect without the application of dye. It is as well to remember that the illusion of a field is largely produced by the provision of suitable hedges, or, in appropriate cases, dry stone walls, with field gates. In fields which are under cultivation it is usual to find a strip of grass, which may be about three feet wide, marching with the hedges on all sides. Little details of this kind help to build up the illusion; there is a lot of suggestion about effective scenic modelling. Fortunately in Britain fields are usually comparatively small in individual extent by comparison with the vast acreages to be found in some overseas countries. Hence there is ample excuse for the introduction of hedges where space for scenic effects is strictly limited.

Fig. 13a shows a field gate, scaled for " OO " gauge. It can be soldered up in a few minutes from $\frac{1}{8}$ in. by $\frac{1}{16}$ in. brass strip. Actually $\frac{1}{8}$ in. strip is rather wide for the purpose and if some $\frac{1}{16}$ in. or 3/32 in. strip can be obtained it would look better. The gate need not be made to open; it can be soldered up with the gate posts all in one piece. Such gates are often left unpainted and the colour of the well weathered timber may, perhaps, be best represented by a brownish grey.

Fig 13a

CHAPTER FOUR

Roads and Waterways

MACADAM roads can be represented quite simply by painting the surface a medium tone of grey. This is obtained by mixing white and black and the addition of a little cobalt is recommended. Either poster colours or matt oils can be used. Road surfaces are never the same tone all over but become darker towards the crown due to the oil dropped by motor vehicles and the soot deposited by exhaust pipes. To secure this effect the reader is advised to pass the brush over the middle part of the surface a second time, with a darker tint, while the first coat is still wet. If this is done carefully the tones will run and blend at the edges so that a progressive darkening is obtained. For the second application the blue may be omitted. Another method, which is simpler to carry out, is to apply charcoal down the centre of the road with a piece of cloth or cotton wool.

Very porous surfaces, such as most of the soft pulpboards, should be treated with size, or wood primer, before any attempt is made to paint them.

It is hardly worth while to go to the trouble of reproducing the camber of a road, and in any case, decent roads do not have a very pronounced camber nowadays. To suggest a country road with the surface in rather poor condition, a sprinkling of silver sand, or pumice powder, can be applied on an adhesive after painting.

Gravel roads are produced by a sprinkling of red sand (or red and silver sand mixed) on a surface which has been painted a light brown or fawn colour. For gravel roads on what is supposed to be chalk soil, as suggested by the presence of chalk pits or cliffs in the locality, a little pumice powder, or actual chalk, can be mixed with the sand.

For a heavily-rutted cart lane we can spread a layer of the Alabastine mix or Pyruma. Before it sets draw a couple of grooves with a pointed stick to represent the ruts formed by cart wheels. Alternatively, a toy vehicle of suitable size can be used for the purpose by pushing it slowly and deliberately along the road once or twice. Apply a wash of brown or fawn paint and sprinkle sand. If the track is supposed to be on clay soil—and very muddy—it can be painted with yellow ochre which has been toned down slightly with a touch of brown, and the sand can be omitted except in the verges. A little clear varnish, run into the ruts with a small brush, will suggest that they are partly filled with water.

Concrete roads are, perhaps, best represented by white matt oil paint with a very little Vandyke brown and black. If anything more seems necessary, the reader can sprinkle a little silver sand, or pumice powder, on Casco glue. In this, as in many other scenic effects, much depends on the nature of the surface ; on a smooth one, such as cardboard or planed wood, the sand may be necessary, but on one which has a natural texture, such as pulpboard, nothing may be gained. The reader is recommended to make one or two experiments on a waste piece of the material which is to be used.

An alternative method of representing concrete would be to apply a thin layer of Pyruma, to smooth it off carefully with a trowel, and leave it as it is. But whichever method is used, a *thin* wash of transparent black over the middle part, where traffic is heaviest, will be an improvement. The reader will have noticed that concrete roads are usually laid in sections, a gap of perhaps a couple of inches being left between adjacent ones and filled with tar or bitumen. This is a useful point, and worthy of inclusion. The length of the sections is about 28 ft. to 30 ft. The lines can be formed with a fine brush and dark grey (not black) paint if the worker's hand is steady enough. It may be suggested that poster colours are easier to manage than oils and can be washed out if the line wobbles, but they will not take properly on all surfaces. Those who feel unable to manage a brush for such fine work might use instead a solid black carbon pencil, sharpened to the best point it will take and frequently touched up on sandpaper. With this the lines can be ruled and there will be no difficulty about keeping them straight. For " OO " gauge the thinner they are the better ; they are likely in any case to be slightly over scale width.

The white lines which often follow the crown of macadam roads should be introduced in appropriate places. In some cases they are

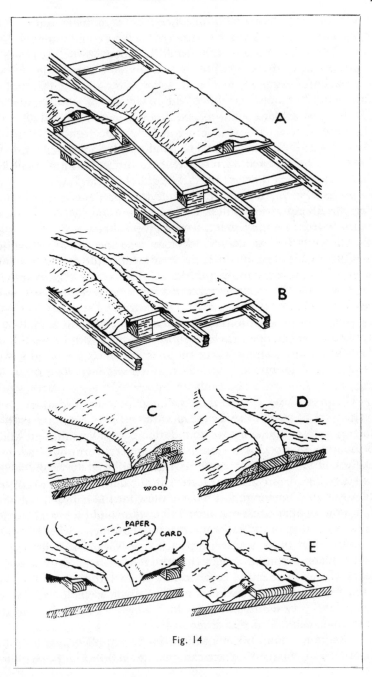

Fig. 14

continuous for considerable distances, but it is more usual to find
them only on bends, and for some yards before and after the bend.
For " OO " gauge the width should be about $\frac{1}{16}$ in. It requires a
steady hand to draw a white line of any considerable length with
a brush but, fortunately for the modeller, it is quite usual for highway
authorities to employ a broken line : sections of white line 2 ft. or
3 ft. long with blank areas of about equal length interposed. This,
of course, is easier to manage successfully. On first-class roads it is
usual to employ a line of metal studs in place of a painted white line.
These can be represented very well by a row of lill pins driven in so
that only the heads are visible. The rubber " cats' eyes," now used
in place of metal studs, are difficult to reproduce in model form.
Perhaps lill pins, used as described above but touched with a slightly
warm-toned light grey paint, would give the effect.

The degree of success which may be expected in modelling a
road depends not so much on the treatment of the road surface itself
as on the discreet handling of details such as white lines and road
signs, and on the working up of the banks and verges. *The truth is
that if these look right almost anything will pass for a road surface.* In Fig.
14 four typical situations are indicated. Diagrams A and B are
applicable to the open table-top form of construction, and C and D
show similar formations where the road is laid on a solid baseboard.
In the first diagram we have a road at a lower level than the adjoining land. The banks are built up by any of the methods described
in Chapter Two : earth-mix, sacking, or crumpled paper, on a
framework of wood or stiff card or wire netting. For small embankments, such as these, a card foundation is usually sufficient and no
framework of wood is required. The general form of construction
is, of course, much the same as that employed for railway track
boards. The boards should have 1 in. or 2 in. of extra width, over
that required for the road itself, to allow for the fixing of the banks.
Crumpled paper can be attached with glue and pins, and the edge
concealed, during the subsequent scenic treatment, with glue, sand,
sawdust, and other scenic properties. In the second diagram the
construction is similar except that the road is banked up above the
level of the surrounding country. For curved sections the board
used for the road surface can be cut with a keyhole saw, or with
one of the very useful saw sets which consist of a handle and three
interchangeable blades of different sizes.

Diagrams C and D show similar layouts applied to a solid baseboard. In C the road surface can be painted direct on the baseboard

and the banks built up by the usual methods. In D the road surface is a strip of wallboard, plywood, etc., as in A and B. Returning to diagram C, it will be clear that if the depth is not very great the banks can be modelled in Alabastine or Pyruma without the interposition of any wood or card framework. It is suggested, however, that odd pieces of wood or wallboard should be tacked to the baseboard to serve as fillers and economise the earth-mix by

A road and level crossing in course of construction. The road surface is a piece of thick card which will be painted grey with poster colours and treated with fine silver sand. Some care was necessary in fitting the section of the road surface between the rails to avoid the risk of fouling the wheels of trains. The straight track on the right is a short industrial siding and will not be extended to cross the road. The card foundation of a grass bank will be seen towards the lower left-hand corner.

avoiding the necessity for building it up to a rather excessive thickness. Fig. 14E is a repetition of Fig. 14, C and D, except that card and crumpled paper are used for the verges instead of an earth-mix.

WATERWAYS

Part of what has been said concerning roads applies also to rivers and canals. The surface of the water will be represented by strips of wallboard, plywood, or thick card, and the banks built up exactly as in Fig. 14, diagrams A and C. Even diagrams B and D would be applicable to those canals in built-up beds which run at a level above that of the surrounding country.

The main difference between a river and a road, from the modeller's point of view, lies in the treatment of the surface to represent water instead of concrete or macadam and in the provision of such details as landing stages, weirs, and waterfalls. The problem, then, is how to represent water, and it must be admitted that a highly realistic representation is not easy to achieve. Nevertheless, a slightly stylised effect which will satisfy all but the most critical, is quite simply arranged. What may be the best method to adopt depends on the worker's confidence in his own powers, and on his skill in the handling of colour. If he has any misgivings in these matters it may be wise to adopt an easy, although less realistic, method, and avoid the risk of an inferior job.

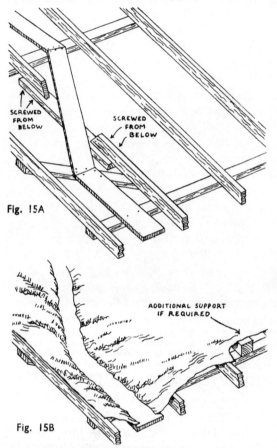

Fig. 15A

Fig. 15B

The writer's own method will be described and we shall then consider more elaborate schemes, for it is hardly possible to devise a single procedure which will suit everyone.

The first job is to install a bed of plywood, Essex board, thick card, or whatever may be available. It should be noted that we use the word " bed " in this sense as a matter of convenience, although what we are representing is not in fact the bed at all but the *surface* of the water, and the reader is asked to keep this in mind. If the waterway is of any considerable extent it is hardly likely that it will be possible to find a single piece of material large enough to form the whole of it in one unbroken section. There will probably have to be one or more butt joins, and they will have to be concealed as best we may. The simplest way is to cover them with strips of stiff paper, applied with paste or some kind of glue. If some form of paint which is mixed with water is to be used it is safer to lay the paper strips with a waterproof adhesive, such as Casco or Durofix, for if this precaution is not taken there is a slight risk that the paper might lift and ruck when soaked with the paint. The writer cuts the edges of the strips with scissors to form a wavy line because this is less likely to be noticeable than a straight one and accords, to some extent, with the idea of ripples and currents. In Fig. 15A sections of the bed are shown nailed to the substructure of the baseboard, and it will be seen that they are depressed to the level of the transverse members in order to bring the river to a lower level than the land adjoining it. This, of course, is a matter governed by the circumstances of the individual case, and would not always apply. Notice the method adopted where the river crosses one of the longitudinal members : a section of the latter has been cut out and another piece of 2 in. by 1 in. timber, somewhat longer than the piece removed, has been screwed underneath to bridge the gap. The bridging piece should be secured with two substantial screws at each end for it becomes an integral part of the baseboard structure. Modifications of this kind are more conveniently made after the substructure has been erected and while " scenicing " and the laying of baseboard sections is in progress. It is not usually advisable to attempt to plan such details in advance ; the writer usually finds that his original intentions undergo some modification while the work progresses. The imaginative faculties seem to be stimulated by the processes of tracklaying and scenicing, and it is at this stage that shortcomings in the original plan become evident. Notice in Fig. 15A also, that a short diagonal member has been added to provide support for a join between two sections of the river bed.

When a river has to be formed on a solid baseboard which is already fixed in place, one is obliged either to build up the adjoining land above baseboard level or to cut out the course of the waterway with a saw of the keyhole type so that the bed can be fixed below the aperture thus formed. The first alternative should be chosen if possible—for obvious reasons. The second is quite practicable where nothing more intimidating than a soft pulpboard is concerned, but for anything harder (wood or semi-hard wallboard) the cutting will be found a slow and laborious business if there is very much of it to be done. The case is aggravated by the fact that a considerable proportion of the cuts must be made in situations where it is difficult

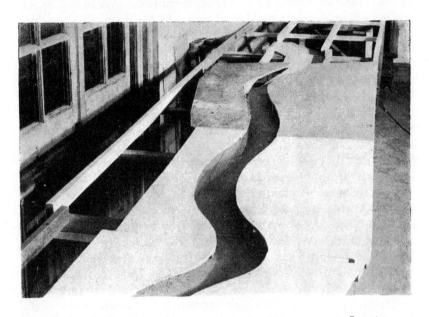

The preliminary construction for the banks of a river, cut in Ensonite board. The river " bed " is in position and the actual banks will be worked up on this foundation with card, paper, and earth-mix. It will be seen that this river runs in a moderately deep gorge. This photograph shows a baseboard of the traditional " all over " type, but it has not been extended to the rear wall (on left) where hills and cliffs are to be erected.

to manipulate the saw properly or to exert normal force on it. The reader is advised to think the matter out very carefully before he commits himself to such an undertaking.

When the bed has been formed it must be treated in some way to suggest the appearance of water, and we have already observed that several methods are available. That used by the writer is to treat the surface with a mixture of sky blue and apple green distemper, the two shades being mixed in approximately equal proportions.

It is inevitable that opinions should differ as to what constitutes an acceptable colour for water, and different batches of distemper might show some variation in depth of tone. Therefore the reader is advised to test a sample of the mixture on a waste piece of material *and to let it dry* so that the effect can be judged before proceeding. If, however, the colour of the first coat is not satisfactory a second can be applied, and may be necessary in any case. The reader is cautioned against using too dark a colour; if necessary a little white distemper could be added. It is hardly necessary to say that the distemper is used in exactly the same manner as for ordinary house decoration ; it should be applied with a distemper brush and worked very much as one works oil paint. That is to say that the brush should be " worked out " by distributing the distemper over as wide an area as possible before picking up a fresh supply.

By the writer's method the next step is to apply sheets of cellophane over the distemper. Ordinary office gum is brushed on the distempered surface, using a 1 in. (or wider) flat brush. The cellophane is very thoroughly crumpled between the hands, carefully opened out, and laid in place on the gum. This will impart something of the sparkle of running water ; the gum will darken the tone of the distemper by several shades and help to produce an impression of depth. It is not desirable for the gum to cover every square inch of the water surface ; if the brush is worked over the surface quickly, so that patches here and there are missed, the resulting variation of tone will give a more satisfactory appearance. The method is illustrated in Fig. 16A where we see the river banks fixed in place so as to overlap the edges of the cellophane.

It is, of course, not essential to lay the cellophane on gum, although the writer has recently favoured that method. It can be laid on the dry surface and will be held in place by the river banks which, as shown in Figs. 15B and 16, overlap it. In this case, however, it is advisable to tack it down with a touch of Durofix here and there to prevent it riding up. And one word of caution must be offered : do not spread the cellophane out too much after it has been crumpled. It has an annoying habit of shrinking and some allowance must be made for this ; if it is laid quite flat it is not unlikely that after a few weeks it will be found to have become quite taut in places, like the skin on a drum, which spoils the effect of running water. Where two sheets of cellophane meet it is recommended that the edges be cut to a wavy line with scissors and arranged to overlap by about 2 in. The overlapping portions should be stuck together by introducing Durofix between them.

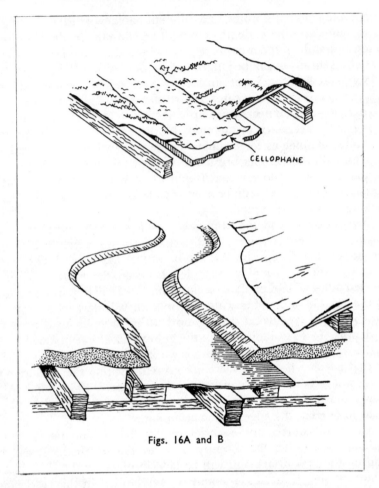

CELLOPHANE

Figs. 16A and B

The only serious drawback to the cellophane method is that if this material becomes torn, or very grubby, it is difficult to replace it without disturbing the river banks, which, as explained above, are built over it. The result is so good in other respects, however, that it is worth while to take a chance on this. It is always possible to patch on top of the original cellophane by cutting a piece with rounded and irregular edges and setting it in place with Durofix, and such patching is practically invisible if carefully done. A point in favour of cellophane is that it seems to offer the only method which will suggest the sparkle of water in a photograph. But this, it must be understood, demands careful photography and lighting ;

a panchromatic emulsion should be used and the minimum correct exposure should be found (if necessary by trial and error) to give maximum value to the high light tones.

An alternative method is to paint the bed with a blue-green oil paint, instead of distemper, and then to apply a couple of rather thick coats of clear decorator's varnish. The kind sold by oil and colour shops for the treatment of furniture and woodwork is quite suitable. This produces a more robust surface than cellophane and it is a simple matter to apply another coat of varnish if it becomes dull after a time. In fact, the more coats which are put on the better, provided each is allowed to dry before the next is applied. Use the brush so that the strokes follow the supposed direction of the current. The oil paint and varnish method is probably the one most used, and the writer has seen very fine results obtained with it. The reader who adopts it should not omit to make a preliminary test of the paint and varnish on a waste piece of the material which is to be used.

Before the war the writer produced a presentable river very simply and quickly by pasting down strips of a light blue wallpaper and covering it with cellophane. The effect was fresh and pleasing although the colour of the paper was totally deficient in green and more suitable for a sky.

It will be clear that when paint or distemper is employed the worker can either play for safety by rendering the waterway an even, unvarying, colour all over, or, given the necessary skill and confidence, he can attempt a more realistic effect by varying the colour to accord with local conditions, blending in browns and deeper greens where the water is shallow or stagnant and in places where the banks are lined with trees which may be assumed to cast a reflection on the surface. For such treatment oil colour is preferable to distemper ; the paints should be used well diluted with turpentine if they are to be made to run together and blend, and it is advisable to make a few experiments on a waste piece of material. The colour of a river may pass through an almost infinite range of gradations, from a mixture of deep green and brown near the banks to a clear sky blue or almost a steel grey in midstream according to the weather conditions prevailing at the moment. Water has no colour of its own but simply takes that of the sky and of any objects which may be reflected in it, although observation will show that the effect is modified both by angle of view and by the degree of surface agitation. There is really no reason why the worker should be afraid to experiment boldly because the result may be better than he anticipates and if it fails it can be covered up with an even coat of greenish blue and no harm will have been done. Foam, on a seashore or a fast-flowing river, can be represented by a stippling motion with a round brush and thick white paint. Very interesting results might be obtained with a spray gun. Even a garden spray might give satisfactory results since a smooth and even effect is not wanted.

A refinement is to lay sand close to the river banks, either before the varnish is applied or while it is wet. This will give the effect of partially submerged banks and shoals. The same device can be applied to stagnant ponds. It may be noted that this treatment can be applied to cellophane covered surfaces as well as to painted ones. If the sand does not have a suitable appearance of wetness a wash of varnish can be applied on top of it. Green sawdust can be used in the same manner to suggest floating weeds and scum. It is hardly necessary to say that in such matters as this local conditions must be considered ; weeds and scum are unlikely to appear in fast-flowing rivers, except in recesses in the banks which form traps for floating matter and against the piers of bridges on the up-stream side. This is a little detail which modellers usually forget ; weeds and scum almost always accumulate around the piers of bridges.

Many workers have made use of sheets of rippled glass, laid on a suitably painted surface, to represent harbour basins and waterways. Unfortunately, this method does not lend itself very readily to the twists and turns of a river, and some difficulty might be encountered in fixing the banks since it is clearly out of the question to obtain a fixing through the glass with tacks or pins in the usual manner. An earth-mix could be laid on the glass without any particular difficulty, but for other forms of ground, such as crumpled paper, it would be necessary to rely on an adhesive. One of the Bostik range would probably be the best for the purpose. A well built and rigid substructure is necessary since some unanticipated pressure, due, perhaps, to warping of the timber, might crack the glass. To guard against this possibility the glass should not be fixed down too rigidly but laid on strips of felt or rubber, or several thicknesses of newspaper.

A refinement of this method is to support the glass so that it is not in contact with the painted bed but raised, perhaps ½ in., above it. This gives an effect of translucence and depth which cannot be equalled by any other means. The bed may be painted in irregular patches of green and brown, changing to a greenish blue in parts where the water is supposed to be deep. Mr. John Allen, of California, has given a description in the *Model Railroader* of how he produced a small timber pier or landing stage when using this method. The supporting piers were made in two parts, one representing the portion below water level and the other the portion above. The first part was built up on the bed of the lake and the glass was then laid on top. The piers were, of course, carefully adjusted to reach up just to the underneath surface. The above-water level part of the landing stage was then constructed on the glass, each timber being carefully lined up with its continuation below the surface.

When a river is bordered by flat and low-lying meadowland the banks can be formed very expeditiously by the method shown in Fig. 16B. A soft pulp board, about ½ in. thick, is cut to the outline of the river with a keyhole saw, *held at a steep angle*. This gives a nice effect of sloping banks with very little working-up, and it is often possible to produce both banks at one sawcut by the simple expedient of turning one of the pieces over. These pieces are nailed over the river bed the desired distance apart and form the basis for subsequent operations. The rough sawn edges should be given a coat of size before any attempt is made to apply paint to them because the open fibres will be found excessively " hungry " and would absorb the paint as fast as it was applied. It will be seen that this method is most easily used in cases where the river is above the transverse members of the substructure (not sunk between them as in Fig. 15) or where there is already an all-over baseboard.

While dealing with waterways we may conveniently consider certain special features such as waterfalls and canal locks. Figs. 17 and 18 show very straightforward methods of constructing a canal lock, and it will be found to be a very attractive and rather unusual scenic feature. The bed of the waterway below the lock will presumably be laid directly on the substructure and the continuation above the lock will be raised on crossbearers of wood. In Fig. 17 the construction is shown if the lock is to be represented with water at the higher level, as when a craft is entering or leaving in the upstream direction, and Fig. 18 illustrates the arrangement with the lock empty. The latter, perhaps, is the more attractive arrangement as it enables more of the lock walls to be shown. The walls of the lock, and of the approaches, are built up in cardboard or thin wood

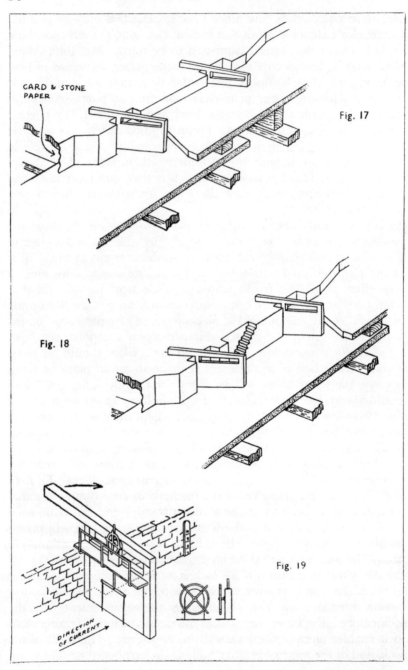

CARD & STONE
PAPER

Fig. 17

Fig. 18

Fig. 19

DIRECTION
OF CURRENT

and stone paper. There should be a flight of steps, leading down into the lock, set back within the face on each side. This is shown in Fig. 18. The gates, Fig. 19, are most conveniently made from ⅛ in. or ₃⁄₁₆ in. plywood and stripwood and should be glued or pinned in position. It will be noted in Fig. 17 that the gates at the lower end are " complete " whereas for the upstream end only the part which is visible at high water level is modelled. The gangways on the gates can be strips of thin wood (1 mm. ply or pipe lighters of a certain

A canal lock constructed by the author exactly as described in this chapter.

kind) or card, secured with Durofix to pins which are forced into the gate and bent up at right angles to form the handrail supports. The sluice operating gear, usually mounted on the gates themselves and designed to be operated from the gangway, is modelled in stripwood and wire. There are several patterns but that shown is probably the simplest to model. The hand wheels should be the equivalent of 2 ft. or 2 ft. 6 in. diameter. They can be small ships' steering wheels from one of the firms which cater for model ship-builders. Alternatively, they might be bent up in wire and the spokes soldered in. The writer once made a presentable set from snap dress fasteners, using the thinner part only and filing out the

the four holes to produce the effect of spokes connecting the rim to the centre. The thing which has the appearance of a rod, projecting upwards out of the top of the mechanism casing, is in reality a length of iron rack, something like a camera rack on a large scale, engaging with a pinion on the wheel shaft. As the wheel is turned the rack rises farther out of the casing and lifts the sluices through

The lock shown here is near Rickmansworth in Buckinghamshire. The gates differ in a few particulars from the type shown in Fig. 19, which was taken from a prototype near Windsor, on the Thames. The huge timber handles, used for working the gates, serve also as gangways for crossing from one side to the other and the iron handrails are located accordingly. A mooring bollard will be noted in the foreground.

the medium of the rods which can be seen below in Fig. 19. The gates are usually a dull brownish black (better represented with water paint than with oils). They should be worked up, more particularly near water level, with thin green paint to represent the slime which adheres to them. The part of the handle which projects over the bank is usually painted white. These handles, by the way, are best made from square section stripwood, tapered slightly with a knife and sandpaper, and secured to the gate with glue and a couple of fine pins. The sluice operating wheels are also white but the rest of the mechanism should be a rusty brownish black.

The other details hardly require comment. The bollards (usually in pairs) can be purchased or turned on a lathe. They can be represented quite well by some kinds of nail, driven into the bank so as to project the scale equivalent of about 18 in. The inevitable notice

The same gates viewed from the opposite direction. The sluice operating gear presents certain differences from the type shown in Fig. 19. Each gate is provided with a horizontal rod which is fitted with pinions and operates in bearings mounted on the upright wooden posts. The pinions engage racks which by their action raise and lower the sluices. The ends of the rods are reduced to form a squared shank over which can be fitted a removable handle, something like a motor car starting handle. Possibly the reason for employing a detachable handle is to discourage unauthorised tampering.

board and a lifebelt stand can be made from $\frac{1}{16}$ in. dowel rod and card or from wire and sheet metal with the aid of solder. Lifebelts might be represented by small rings, but since it never seems to be possible to find one just the right size the writer has always contrived to bend them in 16-gauge copper wire with the assistance of round-nosed pliers. The banks immediately adjoining the lock should be treated as paving stones or cobbles—for which Merco old stone paper may be used—and as gravel. A lock-keeper's cottage and a small garden, or at least a timber hut, should be provided. It is usual for mooring posts to be fixed in the water, close to the banks, above and below the lock for the use of boats which are waiting to enter. A gauge, indicating the height of the water, is fixed to one of the banks below the lock. This is simply a plank about 1 ft. wide, with large figures painted on it giving the height above the river bed in feet. One is shown in the top right-hand corner of Fig. 19. The timber strakes, usually set in the gravel or paving to provide a firmer footing when operating the gate handles, are another detail which should not be omitted. They can be represented by strips

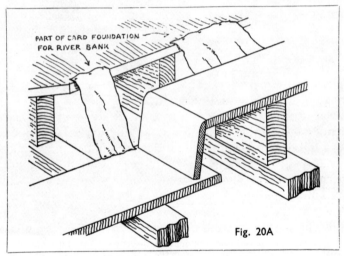

PART OF CARD FOUNDATION
FOR RIVER BANK

Fig. 20A

of card, about 1/16 in. wide for 4 mm. scale, stuck in place and painted a brownish black. There is usually a small landing stage in the vicinity of a lock.

WATERFALLS

A waterfall is another attractive feature which is seldom modelled. In fact the only examples which the writer can recall are in the United States and the method described here is to some extent adapted from one which was described and illustrated in the *Model Railroader* several years ago. It may be pointed out that waterfalls, and locks also, provide a convenient and plausible means for obtaining rapid changes in the level of a river or canal within a restricted space, a consideration which may be of value on

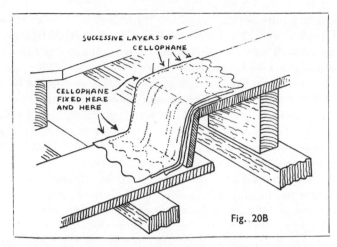

SUCCESSIVE LAYERS OF
CELLOPHANE

CELLOPHANE
FIXED HERE
AND HERE

Fig. 20B

a model railway where two or more track levels are involved and space is usually more or less inadequate. As an example of this a river can be lowered several inches by means of a waterfall to enable a railway track to cross it on a bridge. It seems hardly necessary to mention that a river cannot normally be navigable immediately below a fall. Do not make the mistake of building a landing stage, or a boat house, in a narrow gorge just below a fall where the force of the current would almost certainly render the presence of shipping of any kind impossible.

A waterfall can be made by arranging the upper and lower sections of the river bed in much the same way as has been described

Fig. 20C

in connection with locks. They are connected by a piece of wood, or stiff card, which forms the foundation of the actual fall, and the usual framework of wood and card, or wire netting, is built up to serve as a foundation for the river banks. To this point the procedure should be clear from Fig. 20A. A piece of stiff paper should be glued over the fall ; it should be long enough to overlap at the upper and lower ends by 1 in. or 2 in. The river bed, including the fall, is now painted with blue or blue-green distemper or oil paint, according to which method it has been decided to use. Take a small brush and some white paint, and draw a number of white lines down the fall. They should be quite straight on the fall itself, but not all of the same width and not at a regular distance apart. Some of them can break off part of the way down and some need not reach up to the top. The more irregular they are in this respect the better. There should be a larger area of white at the foot of the fall than at the top to help create the illusion of spray. The effect will be improved if they finish with a " squiggle " on the horizontal surface at the foot of the fall to suggest the turbulence of the water, and the reader should try to finish them off with an almost dry brush so that they trail off to nothing at a distance of perhaps 2 in. or 3 in. from the foot. I have had to describe this in some detail and perhaps, by implication, given it more prominence than it deserves. In reality it is quite unnecessary to go to much trouble at this stage because the work will be largely concealed by the subsequent proceedings. Next cut a strip of cellophane, somewhat wider than the fall to allow for crumpling and long enough to overlap the top and the foot by 1 in. or 1½ in. Cut the ends to a wavy line, as described at an earlier point in this book and shown in Fig. 20B. Crumple it thoroughly and smooth it out as much as possible, and paint a few more parallel white lines on it. It is best to use an oil colour here because poster colours do not take very kindly on cellophane. Secure it in place with Durofix so that it is drawn quite taut over the fall. Leave it free on the actual fall and stick it at the top and bottom. A single layer of cellophane is hardly sufficient to produce a convincing effect, so a second one should be added on top of the first. This one should be cut an inch or two longer than the first so that its ends come in different positions. It can be given a few white lines like the other piece. There is no harm whatever in the addition of further layers of cellophane, up to as many as five or six ; in fact the effect will be improved thereby. The intention is to give an effect of depth to the water. The blue of the foundation should remain faintly visible through the cellophane, and the successive white lines, and if the work has been done with discretion the white and blue will blend to produce a very satisfactory effect. We get an impression of the water breaking into spray and of the play of light on the surface. A little trouble must be anticipated in persuading the cellophane to assume the required position ; it must be smoothed down with the fingers occasionally until it is evident that the adhesive has set sufficiently to prevent further movement. If the top layer can be induced to form a few vertical rucks or pleats so much the better.

A high-level view of the waterfall which appears in the photograph on page 29.

If the river surface is being covered with cellophane one continues, above and below the fall, by overlapping more of it to cover the edges of that on the fall itself. If the alternative method with a clear varnish is used, the varnish should be brushed liberally over the edges of the cellophane and even over the fall. I do not recommend this, however, unless the varnish is very clear and colourless as it may produce some degradation of tone in the one place where it is not wanted.

It may be noted here that a writer in the *Model Railroader* has described a different method of making a waterfall. A little clear varnish was poured over the fall every evening for about a week, and allowed to trickle down. In this manner a considerable depth was gradually built up.

It remains to build up the river banks with the Alabastine mix or by any of the methods described in an earlier chapter. It may be supposed that outcroppings of bare rock with patches of rather lush vegetation will form the dominant motif. Pieces of actual rock may be used in a setting of the earth-mix, and this may be the best way for those who do not feel too sure of their rock colours. Rocks near water level, and very close to the fall, should be brushed with clear varnish to give them a wet appearance from the spray and should be rather darker in tone than dry rock. They are likely to assume a greenish tinge from the presence of the mosses which flourish under moist conditions. This should be suggested (preferably before any varnish is applied) by applying green paint which has been thinned sufficiently to do little more than tint the surface and allows the ground colour to show through in patches. In producing such effects it is difficult to judge the result except by trial and error. You cannot tell what the effect will be by a preliminary test on an odd piece of material because so much depends upon form and the influence of adjacent colours. It is advisable, therefore, to avoid overdoing it at first, and to return to the attack, if necessary, after the result has been considered.

The finishing touch is to add the boulders which are usually found, partially submerged, at the foot of a waterfall. The reader will find that some of the larger pieces of gravel which can always be picked up in a garden have one side which is practically flat, as if they had been split along a fracture line. It is these which should be selected for this purpose, and the most useful ones will have a diameter of from ½ in. to 1 in. They should be washed and set in place with Durofix, the flat side, of course, being downwards. Finally add a few touches of matt white oil paint around the foot of the fall and in the spaces between the boulders to complete the effect of foam and spray. A few more stones may be placed at random a little farther down stream and should be touched with green paint and with varnish, particularly on the side facing upstream. This will represent the slime which is carried by the water and adheres to any obstruction in the path of the current. This, it may be added, is hardly likely to occur to any considerable extent immediately at the foot of the fall because the turbulence of the water there would be too great to permit anything to be left behind; the rock is subjected to a constant scouring action.

Building a river bridge with card, wood, and printed stone paper. This photograph shows the method of construction with only one of the sides in position.

BEACHES

A feature which may be mentioned in this chapter is sandy beaches. Where cellophane is used it should be cut away from the area which is to represent the beach. Apply almost any adhesive to the surface, working up to the line where the beach disappears below water level. If cellophane is used allow the adhesive to lap over it for about half an inch. Now sprinkle red or silver sand heavily until the area is completely covered. The sand can be

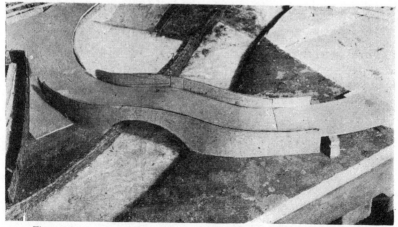

The work is carried a stage further. The second card side has been added.

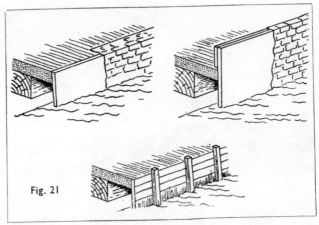

Fig. 21

made to appear wet by a coat of clear varnish.   If the beach is to slope down towards the water, a thin layer of the earth-mix, of graduated thickness, can be arranged and the sand laid on top of it, or a piece of thin card can be cut to the required shape and stuck to the baseboard with card or thin wood packing along the landward edge to give it a slight tilt.

To reproduce convincingly the plants which grow on the surface of stagnant water is not very easy.   The best method the writer knows is to treat the surface with Durofix and to sprinkle green dyed sawdust rather sparingly.   A few scraps of artificial moss might be added with discretion.   Water lilies might be suggested by circles of green paper, cut with a leather punch.   If several were laid so as to overlap the fact that they were not quite the right shape would not be obvious.

The writer has modelled the tall flags which grow close to the banks of slow rivers by cutting up some pieces extracted from a brush type pot scourer into lengths of about ¾ in.   Each one of these was planted separately in a hole formed in the surface of the

Fig. 22

The bridge and its surroundings completed.

river with the point of a scriber, after being touched with Durofix. They were arranged to stand about $\frac{1}{4}$ in. to $\frac{3}{8}$ in. above the surface, and painted a yellow-green when in place. The result was quite pleasing, but could hardly be said to justify the relatively enormous amount of work involved to produce anything like a decent display.

Built-up harbour and canal walls do not require much explanation, and the three diagrams in Fig. 21 are practically self-explanatory. The foundation of the wall can usually be thick card, pinned in position, and the surface can be represented by one of the printed stone papers as in A and B. When a parapet is added it may be advisable to stick another layer of card behind, as in B, to build up a reasonable thickness. The stone paper should always be worked up with green paint, especially near water level, to represent the slime which accumulates. This is one of the finishing touches which really count in the final effect and should not be omitted, and a little varnish sparingly applied will do no harm ; it will give the stone a wet appearance.

Fig. 21C shows a timber harbour wall, made by scribing the card to represent planks and with upright retaining and rubbing posts of stripwood. It is finished with a mixture of black and brown paint (perhaps with a touch of white added), and then worked up with green as described above. The posts are sometimes painted white to be visible at night.

Fig. 22 shows the construction of a flight of water steps. The steps can be cut from solid wood with a fine saw or built up from strips of diminishing length and glued together as shown on the right.

This chapter may conclude with a few notes on the subject of bridges, considered as part of the scenic work. The sequence of three photographs on pages 63 and 65 show the erection in wood and card of a road bridge over a river. In the first photograph we see the rough foundation of the bridge in course of construction, and with one of the sides in place. The road surface is cut from thick card and tacked over wood supports of varying height. The arch is another piece of card, just sprung into place between the wood supports which form the abutments.

In the second photograph the side of the bridge nearest to the camera has been added. Its shape was found by the simple expedient of holding a piece of card hard up against the bridge and running a pencil along the edge of the road surface, and also round the underside of the arch. For this the pencil was held through the arch from the far side. With the aid of these pencil

The first stage of the construction of a road bridge spanning a railway. The method is essentially the same as in the three foregoing photographs.

Another interesting example of bridge construction. The hedges give an idea of what can be accomplished with a loofah cut into narrow strips.

lines it was a simple matter to cut the card (with scissors) to produce a parapet of even height above the road surface. The parapet on the side farthest from the camera has been thickened by another layer of card, made up, as a matter of convenience, from several small pieces.

In the third photograph, page 65, the work has been completed with stone paper and a coping added to the parapets. The road has been painted grey and sprinkled with sand, and the river banks worked up with sand and green sawdust.

The photograph on page 66 shows the first stage in the construction of a road bridge over a railway. The card road surface is tacked to wood blocks as in the preceding illustrations and the bridge was worked up with stone paper in a similar manner.

The photograph on this page, shows another bridge, of generally similar construction, complete. Note the loofah hedges in the background.

CHAPTER FIVE

Afforestation

SEVERAL materials have been used with more or less success to make trees and hedges and which of them the reader selects may depend on the nature of the materials which can be most easily obtained. I shall indicate the most popular methods and leave the reader to make his own choice. It should be made clear, however, that there is no need to adhere throughout to any one method, for trees made from several of the materials mentioned in this chapter can be mixed freely, and there will be nothing incongruous about the result. In fact trees differ so much in form and colour that the modeller can never hope to rival the diversity of nature ; it is as well to experiment with as many materials as possible, and never to judge any tree a failure until it has been actually tried out on the model landscape in conjunction with others. Even poor examples can be made serviceable by discreetly grouping them so that they are partly concealed from view by better ones.

Preference should be given to those methods which enable trees to be produced quickly and in bulk rather than one at a time. They should usually be made in batches of half-a-dozen or a dozen. It is simply not worth while to spend the better part of an evening laboriously producing one or two, because at that rate you will become bored with the job long before the landscape is adequately afforested. A really generous use of trees, even if they are of mediocre workmanship, will produce a more satisfactory result than a niggardly application of more perfect ones, for, above all things, the countryside should not look barren and starved of vegetation.

The materials most used for trees and hedges are given below with indications as to their use.

RUBBERISED HORSEHAIR

We may deal with this first because in the writer's estimation it is the most convenient and generally useful. There appear to be two grades, designated respectively as yellow and black. Either may be used, but the first named is to be preferred. This material is manufactured by Xetal Products Ltd., Long Eaton, Nottingham. It is used for upholstery purposes and the reader might be able to secure an adequate supply for his purposes by obtaining the left-over pieces from an upholsterer. Otherwise an enquiry could be addressed to the manufacturers.

The method of using it is to start by cutting pieces to resemble the forms of trees, as nearly as possible, with stout scissors. The reader can exercise his ingenuity in attempting to reproduce the characteristic forms of certain kinds, recalling, for example, the well rounded top and spread towards the base of oaks, the " waist " which is usually observable in elms, and would be most easily re-presented by two pieces of the material fixed one above the other, and the tall, rather coned, form of fir trees. To supplement such variations of shape the reader can make observations of the various colours of foliage, as seen from a distance, and attempt to suggest them by the careful mixing of oil colours or by the use of different grades of dyed sawdust.

The trunks can be twigs or small branches from the garden, with the bark left on. The end which is to be inserted into the tree should be roughly pointed with a pocket knife, smeared with adhesive, and pushed well into the foliage. To provide leaves the writer's practice is to brush the tree all over with office gum, or other adhesive, and to sprinkle liberally with sawdust. It is ad-visable to keep the sawdust in a flat tin and to hold the tree over it, so that the surplus is not wasted, but falls back into the container We can use either dyed sawdust or the undyed kind and paint it with oil colour when the adhesive has dried. The writer prefers the first alternative.

It should be remembered that dyed sawdust gives a more delicate and tree-like texture than can be expected from paint. If paint is used, however, mix a medium green (decorator's matt colour or undercoating will do), a bright clean yellow, and perhaps a little black. The paint should be used well diluted and with a fairly large soft brush. A flat one, ½ in. to 1 in. across, is quite suitable. No attempt should be made to force the paint very deeply between the fibres ; if the external surfaces are lightly tipped it should be sufficient to give the desired effect, and the unpainted parts of the fibres below the surface will suggest the branches. The advantage of yellow over black rubberised horsehair will be evident for the former is not really yellow, but more of a light brown, which is a suitable colour to represent branches and stems wherever it may be visible through the green. If any bare patches have been left by inadvertence they can be painted afterwards, but with the yellow kind this is less necessary than with the black. Do not use the paint too thickly or the result will be rather coarse and matted, not at all suggestive of the delicate texture of foliage.

Trees are planted by the simple expedient of pushing the foot of the trunk, which has been slightly tapered, into a hole drilled in the baseboard or formed with the point of an awl. So long as it is a reasonably tight fit there is no need to secure the tree with adhesive ; it is better not to do so for you may want to shift it to another position at some time with the minimum of damage or disturbance to the scenic work. If, however, a tree occupies a rather prominent position where it is sure to catch the eye, it may be worth while to run a little adhesive round the base of the trunk and to apply green sawdust to give the illusion that it is actually growing out of the soil. The writer usually contrives to conceal the bases of trees with hedges or undergrowth.

SPONGE AND LOOFAH

These are employed in almost exactly the same manner as rubberised horsehair. Sponges are rather light in colour for this purpose, and should be dipped in a weak brown dye, preferably after being cut up into tree shapes so that the dye can penetrate more effectively. The exact strength or colour of the dye is not important, and an immersion of about a minute is quite sufficient, as the sponge is very absorbent. The dye is only intended to provide an undertone and will be almost hidden by the foliage in any case. A flat teaspoonful of almost any brown dye, of one of the popular domestic brands, in two or three pints of water should serve the purpose. Drying is rather slow and the sponge should be put in a warm place, near a stove or radiator, if possible.

Loofah will be improved if it is similarly treated, although dyeing seems to be rather less important with it. It should be allowed to remain in the dye bath for a longer period, say five minutes, as it is less absorbent than sponge. These materials can be treated with sawdust, dyed or undyed, in exactly the same manner as rubberised horsehair.

STEEL WOOL

This material makes very good trees, but it should be kept away from steel tools, as far as possible, and in no circumstances should it be allowed anywhere near permanent magnet motors. This, of course, means while it is being cut and worked up ; it should be harmless after it has been set with adhesive, etc. It seems that all steel tools are in some degree magnetic, and if they come near to newly cut steel wool they will be found to be covered with metallic " whiskers." The result if this metallic swarf gets between the

WIRE PASSED
THROUGH STEEL
WOOL AND LOOPED
BACK

Fig. 23

pole pieces and armature of a motor can be very exasperating. The method of use is the same as with rubberised horsehair, sponge, or loofah: sawdust is applied with gum, but in this case it is necessary to make sure that the steel wool is completely covered or an unnatural metallic glint will be seen through the foliage. This could no doubt be overcome by dabbing the material with sloppy brown paint before use. for the trunk a twig can be employed as already described, but an alternative method is to use a piece of stranded copper wire, and to fan out the individual wires at the upper end to form boughs and branches, as in Fig. 23. I do not refer to ordinary lighting flex which is not thick enough, or sufficiently rigid, but to 7/22 cable, used for permanent wiring, or something similar. If an insulated wire is used the covering should be left intact on the part which represents the trunk ; if not the trunk should be tinned all over with a soldering bit to present a better surface for paint, or bound tightly with thread. It may be noted that the trunks of growing trees more often appear a brownish *grey* to the eye rather than a full brown.

The steel wool can be cut with sharp tinsnips or dragged apart with the fingers. It should be rolled and worked into appropriate shapes for masses of foliage. It may be found that it tends to open out and refuses to stay in the required shape. If this happens the

A group of trees made of rubberised horsehair, loofah, and steel wool. The production of painted backdrops, as seen here, is discussed in Chapter VIII.

simplest cure is to push a short piece of thin wire through it and to bend over the ends on the outside to hold it together. If the trunk is made of stranded cable a little ball of the material should be attached with adhesive to each of the strands. The wire is pushed through the steel wool, and then looped back so that the mass of foliage is effectively hooked in place as in Fig. 23. When all the foliage is in place the " branches " can be bent so that the lumps of steel wool arrange themselves in a natural manner.

Some workers have tinted steel wool green by dipping it in a tin containing diluted green oil paint. It sounds a rather messy procedure to the writer, and if the reader should decide to attempt this method he is advised in the first place to lay down a large number of sheets of newspapers on the floor and on the table or bench, for the paint has a sinister habit of getting everywhere where it is not wanted.

ARTIFICIAL MOSS

Certain kinds of " artificial " or preserved moss can be used. These are self-coloured in more or less acceptable shades of green, although whether the colour can be regarded as permanent the

72

writer is not prepared to say. These materials require more skill and discretion on the part of the worker than those described in preceding sections. Success depends very much on personal touch, and it is therefore difficult to give explicit directions. The general method can be similar to that suggested for steel wool : use stranded electric cable for the trunk and carefully divide the moss into tufts of appropriate size. If the tufts show a disposition to fall to pieces they may be bound with fine flower wire, or a little adhesive may be dabbed on them and allowed to set. The tufts can be glued to the strands of cable, and it is usually advisable to twist the end of the wire round the moss to hold it more securely in place. With this in mind the wire boughs should be cut about an inch longer than the actual length which it is anticipated will be wanted ; the surplus can be cut off when the tufts have been safely fixed. At any points where it may assume an undesirable prominence the wire can be concealed by a touch of green paint, or by gum and green sawdust.

It must be admitted that the preserved moss method is slower than the others described here, and the writer doubts if the results are likely to justify the extra work.

SEAMOSS

Another useful material is known by the name of seamoss. This is a natural plant of very fine and delicate texture. It is obtainable from Messrs. Woolworths in all the larger towns, but not in the smaller branch stores, or from Killick Model Railway Productions, Crowborough, Sussex. The sprays can be cut apart with scissors and used to represent bushes and young trees in 4 mm. scale. It is only necessary to make a hole in the baseboard with an awl or scriber, and to insert the end of the stem with a touch of adhesive. No colour treatment is required. Larger trees could be produced by using stranded electric cable for the trunk, as described earlier in this chapter, and attaching several sprays to the fanned out wires with glue. Arranged in symmetrical rows the sprays would give a nice representation of a plantation. In miniature scales, such as 2 mm. or $\frac{1}{16}$ in. to the ft., the individual sprays would serve as full-size trees, rather suggestive of fir trees, and would probably prove to be the most satisfactory material for the purpose in these scales. It would be quite possible, if rather laborious, to produce a hedge by " planting " a row of the sprays close together and trimming the tops approximately level with scissors.

The writer finds that excellent trees can be made from the

stalks of bunches of grapes in conjunction with steel wool. Cut irregular tufts of the latter about ¾ in. to 1½ in. long. Fluff them up a little with the fingers if the material is too tightly compacted. Smear the twigs or shoots (or whatever they are called) from which the grapes hung with an adhesive, preferably, I think, Durofix, and allow it about a minute to get tacky. Use the adhesive rather liberally; it will strengthen the rather fragile shoots. Press the tufts of steel wool on to the shoots so that each tuft adheres to at least two or three of them. When the adhesive is dry, dab gum all over the steel wool and sprinkle it with green sawdust. If any patches of the steel wool are visible when the gum has set, conceal them with more sawdust or with touches of green, or brown, oil paint. No doubt sprigs cut from other plants or bushes could be used in the same way. This method of tree-making has distinct possibilities and it is not unduly laborious.

The greatest enemy of all miniature afforestation is dust ; it accumulates gradually, and gives the landscape a dead and dried up appearance. The owner may not become conscious of this for a long time, because the process is so slow that the eye is able to become accustomed to a progressive deterioration. It produces a stronger impression on the occasional visitor who views the scenic work with a fresh vision. It seems that the only really effective remedy is to borrow the vacuum cleaner periodically ; brush methods are slow and produce only a partial cure. Do not forget to remove any small objects, such as human figures or porters' trolleys, before bringing the vacuum cleaner too close or they will probably vanish into the nozzle ! It is a bad thing to get into the habit of working in an atmosphere of dust and shabbiness, and dust is one of the worst enemies of satisfactory running of electrically powered model locomotives.

We may add to the foregoing review of tree materials, that many workers in America make use of a substance known as Norwegian lichen. This is a natural plant which appears—to judge from samples which the author has seen—to have been treated with a preserving agent, presumably to render the colour permanent. It makes up readily into very presentable trees, but is not available, as far as the writer knows, in this country.

HEDGES

Bushes and hedges are made of the same materials as trees, and generally by similar methods. Rubberised horsehair, loofah,

and steel wool, can all be cut into long strips, wide enough to stand
$\frac{1}{2}$ in. to $\frac{3}{4}$ in. high (for 4 mm. scale), using strong scissors or tinsnips.
Sponge is less suitable, but can be used for individual bushes. The
usual method of attachment to the baseboard is to run a little
adhesive on to the underside of the hedge and to insert ordinary
pins through it at intervals. The pins should be driven in with a
centre punch so that the heads are concealed within the foliage.
If any of them still catch the eye they can be touched with paint,
or adhesive and green sawdust. If the upper $\frac{1}{4}$ in. of the pin is
bent over with small pliers it will form a hook and hold the material
more securely as in Fig. 24.

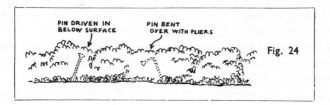

Fig. 24

Hedges, in the right places, seem to pull a model landscape
together, and nothing gives roads such a thoroughly " roadlike "
atmosphere as hedges to mark the verges. And they are less
trouble to make than satisfactory fences. They should be planted
to mark the boundaries between fields and other properties. It is
important to preserve a proper sense of the scale in which one is
working. In " OO " gauge, for example, $\frac{3}{4}$ in. represents about
4 ft. 6 in., which is a fair average height.

It is an excellent idea to brush a rather thick adhesive, such as
Casco, up to the bases of hedges and to apply green sawdust. It
helps to give the impression that the hedge is rooted in the ground.
If necessary a little of the earth-mix can be worked in under the
hedge for the same purpose.

Rough scrub and undergrowth can be represented by snipping
rubberised horsehair with scissors and glueing it directly to the
ground. It is then treated with glue and sawdust or with paint.
An alternative material which gives excellent results is brown
carpet underlay, or some similar coarse felt. Typewriter mats are
similar in composition and texture and one of them could be broken
up to provide a lot of material. As far as possible, the felt should

be pulled apart with the fingers, and not cut, in order to give irregular edges. Small or large pieces can be glued to the ground and worked up with sawdust and paint as already described. The brown colour of the felt should be allowed to show through the foliage in places as it is just the right colour for branches and dead leaves, and will give variety to the surface. The surface should be teased up in places with a comb to avoid an even and " all-overish " effect. For the best result the reader is advised to use at least two shades of green paint or dyed sawdust, and to allow them to blend freely, for the more irregular and diversified the effect may be the better. In the kind of terrain we are considering, different plants are usually mingled and fighting one with another. Differences in the composition of the soil, the presence of rock below the surface, and of water channels or underground streams, will all produce differences in the manner of growth, which may affect the colour and tone of the foliage. In the vicinity of human habitations, the remains of old walls or the foundations of buildings below the surface soil will have a similar effect.

Casco glue is perhaps preferable to ordinary gum for use on felt ; the latter, being very thin and watery, may tend to sink in and mat up the fibres rather more than is desirable. Excellent effects can be obtained by tearing holes in the felt, after it has been glued in place and the adhesive has set, with a screwdriver or some other tool. One can plant tufts of rubberised horsehair or loofah on top of the felt to suggest bold plants which have forced their way up above the general level.

We may return for a moment to the subject of trees to point

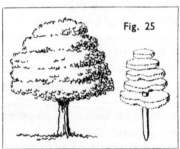

Fig. 25

out that it is possible to represent some of the smaller kinds by cutting and tearing several roughly shaped circles of felt and sticking them one on top of another to form a pile as in Fig. 25. The upper layers would diminish in size to give the rounded shape of the top and the foliage treatment would be as described in the preceding paragraphs. The trunk would pass through the pile and hold it together.

A pleasant variation of colour could be introduced into undergrowth and scrub by the representation of patches of heather. How best to produce a " heather mixture " with paints is bound to be a matter of individual opinion, but the writer thinks that a mixture of red and blue (vermilion with cobalt rather than ultramarine) with the addition of a little white should be quite satisfactory. When dry it might be flecked with brown and black to suggest the bracken which is usually found with heather.

Gorse bushes can be similarily represented by an application of thick matt yellow paint (gamboge, for example), working lightly over the tops of the fibres. For such effects the brush should be used with a not too heavy hand for gorse is only yellow on the surface and there is a mass of brown and green below. To suggest this the material should not be saturated with the yellow paint ; the browns and greens should show through. Perhaps the best way is to apply a dark olive green first, and then to add the yellow.

The impediment to working from nature, for readers who are unused to mixing colours, is that they are likely to have difficulty in reproducing the tones which have been seen. The only solution, of course, is to experiment freely, remembering that the tones of nature appear to vary so much under different conditions of light and at different seasons that exact matching is hardly possible. You cannot hope to match something which is itself variable, and there is no need to attempt to do so. It should be remembered that it is almost always necessary to add a little white to colours ; it provides the most convenient and usual means of softening them, and simulates that slight greying which is produced by distance. Often a very small quantity of black can be added as well ; it will tend to turn greens towards olive.

Only a very broad effect, a massing of colour, is wanted. One usually views a model rather as the real countryside would be seen from a low flying aeroplane, and this fact should be kept in mind. If you have found some detail or a patch of country which you hope will provide inspiration, walk a hundred yards or so away from it, getting on to higher ground if possible. Then try to separate in your mind what you can actually see from what you only think you can see, because you know it is there from previous closer examination. This is a good training in the art of concentrating on essentials. It will give you an idea of how much to include and there could hardly be a better exercise in the art of seeing. Detail which is not noticeable at a hundred yards is usually not worth worrying about.

CHAPTER SIX

Creating a Landscape

IN preceding chapters we have discussed the methods and materials used in scenic modelling : baseboards and preparation of the ground, afforestation, hills, and the like. We can now consider specific applications of the foregoing. When space is severely restricted the " scenicing " may of necessity resolve itself into little more than a narrow background area between the tracks and the walls of the room. Even in these circumstances it is surprising how much can be done if full advantage is taken of such space as there may be. To demonstrate this, the series of drawings numbered 26, 27, 30, and 32, has been prepared to a uniform scale and offers suggestions for treatment in " OO " gauge of a section of baseboard measuring 6 ft. long by 2 ft. wide, avoiding the use of flat painted scenery. This has been done deliberately, because many people mistrust their artistic abilities and are convinced that they could never undertake anything of the nature of landscape painting. The subject will be discussed in a later chapter, where it is hoped to show that the difficulties are not quite so formidable as they may appear, but for the moment we shall limit ourselves to solid three-dimensional work. These drawings comprise a plan and a sketch to suggest the type of effect which might be produced, and also a couple of sections. These last are rather revealing as they show how space can be conserved by the use of some degree of deliberate fore-shortening, or what may be called false perspective. False perspective is, of course, used extensively in the theatre and cinema studio, and in most exhibition and display models. We can employ the principle, to a moderate extent which will serve our purpose, in a quite unscientific manner, and without acquiring any special knoweldge or skill, artistic or otherwise. Fig. 26 provides a simple

78

example of what is implied. The two sections reveal that the hills which form the background are in reality considerably steeper than they would be in nature. But if the colours are handled with a little discretion, to help establish the illusion that the more distant planes are farther away than in reality they are, the fact need not be so obvious as the reader may suppose. The rule for creating the feeling of distance is quite simple and easy to apply : *the colours used on the more distant planes should be somewhat lighter in tone, and perhaps less brilliant, than those used in the foreground.* The colours of distant objects appear not only lighter, but also more grey than those of near ones, and the inexperienced worker will obtain this effect most easily by mixing a little white, and perhaps a trace of black, with his greens and browns, and other colours. The explanation is, of course, that white and black produce grey. By mixing them with any colour you give it a greyish tinge, *and if the white predominates strongly over the black you necessarily lighten the colour at the same time.* The reader is advised to spend a few minutes experimenting on an odd piece of material, mixing various proportions of white and black with the colours he is using for foreground work and noting the result. The idea may sound rather startling, if it is new to the reader, but it is really very simple ; the reader will be able to learn all he wants to know in order to make a start in less than half an hour. When he feels that he can form an idea as to how much modification of the colour is wanted, he should try it out on a section of the actual scenery. If the result does not seem satisfactory, it is better to leave it alone for two or three days and carry on with something else. Then reconsider the matter, and if the effect still seems unsatisfactory go over the work again, modifying the proportions of the colours as may seem advisable. It follows that the proportion of white (or grey) should be increased progressively as the planes recede farther from the standpoint of the observer. That is the theoretical position, but in practice there is certainly no need to be very precise or meticulous about it. In most cases it will probably be sufficient to establish two areas of tone : one for the foreground and middle distance and one for the distance. Naturally, however, the transition from one to the other should not be too obvious ; the worker who lacks confidence in the use of colour can do a lot to conceal the transition, by the use of lines of trees, stone walls, hedges, and similar features. In Fig. 26, for example, we might use full strength foreground colours as far as the trees in the middle distance, which are introduced

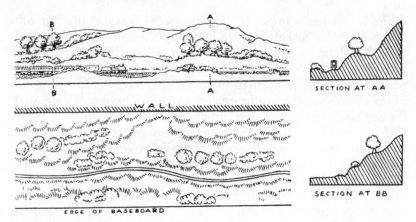

SECTION AT AA

SECTION AT BB

EDGE OF BASEBOARD

Fig. 26

largely to create a sense of separation into planes. From here to the skyline one degree of tone should suffice, although two, carefully blended, would no doubt produce a better effect. It will be seen from this that we may hope to obtain the desired effect by nothing more intimidating than separating the landscape into two areas. The slight dip in the ground level (see section AA), also helps to create the illusion of distance, and of separation between near and far. Those readers who are already experienced in the mixing of colours, and have definite ideas on the subject, might in certain cases obtain better results by the use of blue rather than white or grey, but blue is a distinctly tricky colour to play with, and I feel sure that the inexperienced worker will obtain better results with grey. That is a personal opinion, however, and anyone who feels inclined to experiment with other methods should certainly do so ; he will at least acquire experience and confidence thereby, even if the result should not be entirely successful. And as unsuccessful work can always be painted over no serious risk is incurred.

It will be appreciated that the dyed sawdust method does not lend itself very readily where this technique is to be employed. It should be possible to use two or three grades of sawdust, dyed to different tones, but the writer thinks that oil or tempera paint would be more satisfactory, at least for the final tinting and touching up, since it is easier to control its tone. One method would be to use dyed sawdust of a single colour over background as well as foreground and then to work over it, where necessary, with paint of a colder colour. Some interesting effects might be obtained by using oil colours for the foreground, and tempera colours for the background. Tempera colours have a rather cold pastel quality, which it should be possible to utilise very effectively, but this obviously calls for some experience and artistic feeling. Where sufficient space is available to permit an attempt to be made to suggest distant hills, it might be expedient to omit the sawdust treatment in the extreme distance. The purpose of the sawdust is to suggest grass, and we are not conscious of grass as a definite texture beyond a certain distance, but only of colour. It would be better to apply something of much finer texture, such as silver sand, but it may be found that near the horizon line paint alone, on a suitable surface, will give the best effect. It follows that as far as may be practicable trees and hedges should also be graded, the lighter ones being used farther back. The writer's usual method with bushes and hedges is to paint them, or at least to touch them up, *in position.*

The reader who feels tempted to try this method of suggesting distance may still feel rather uneasy about the problems which appear to arise where the transition is effected from warmer to slightly colder colours. He may think that his skill is not equal to concealing it. The answer is don't worry, and don't meet difficulties of that kind half way. Such things always sound more confusing and intimidating when an attempt is made to describe them in words than they are in reality—and the required difference of tone is actually very slight. Suppose you are working up a hillside : use a large brush and cover the foreground parts first. Then take up some colour of a slightly colder tone which is ready

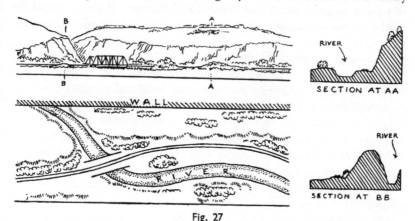

Fig. 27

prepared and carry on, working backwards and forwards over colour already laid to obtain mixing and some degree of gradation.   It is not difficult, and the least experienced worker can hardly go wrong, even at a first attempt.   By the time you have worked up nearly to the skyline you may decide that you can afford to pause, and add a little more white to your paint.   It should be remembered that oil and tempera colour does not dry so quickly as poster colour, and that you will have plenty of time to stop and consider without running the risk of getting high-water marks.   In any case, nobody expects the greens of nature to be quite even and uniform over large areas, and it is in all cases desirable to mix different shades to obtain a more natural result.   This technique is the exact opposite of house painting, for example, where usually an even surface and tone are desired.

Fig. 27 suggests a similar type of country, but a river has been introduced and the railway crosses it by a small bridge.   Section *BB*, considered in conjunction with the plan demonstrates how a river (or a road) can be conducted gracefully " off stage " by arranging for it to disappear behind an outlying spur of the hills so that the point where it ends in the background wall is concealed from normal viewpoints.   This, it may be noted, is a convenient device to avoid the necessity for flat painted scenery, for if the river met the wall in full view one would be obliged to show its continuation in some fashion.   Flat scenery would be the only solution. Perhaps the " isometric " drawing, Fig. 28, will convey the idea better.

The reader is invited to notice in Fig. 27 how use has been made of bushes to help break the skyline and to conceal the fact that the land does not continue normally over the brow of the hill, but comes to an abrupt end.

The pair of photographs on page 83 shows a similar method applied to a road which has to be conducted " off stage."   The upper photograph shows the scene from a normal viewing position. A car will be noted approaching the point where the road disappears behind a bank and trees.   The signpost contributes in that it emphasises the idea of a road junction.   In the lower photo the camera has been raised up so that it is as nearly overhead as was practicable with an ordinary camera stand, and the front pointed downwards.   The car is in the same position as in the first photograph.   It is now evident that the road stops abruptly where it meets the background wall, but to observe the fact it would be

The pair of photographs on this page shows the realisation of the road junction layout depicted in plan in Fig. 29.

necessary to stand on a table, or on the baseboard itself ; the camera
was quite close to the ceiling of the room when this photograph was
taken.   It is, of course, true that in this particular case a freize of
scenery painted on card has been used to assist the effect, but by
moving the road junction about 4 in. to the left, and extending the
screen of trees by a corresponding distance the need for this could
have been avoided.   A plan of this piece of scenic work is given
in Fig. 29.

In Fig, 30, we have a scene in which a village against a hill
background is the principal feature. Some trees are indicated

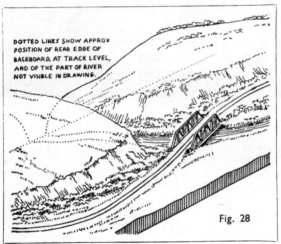

behind the cottages
to isolate the back-
ground and make
the hills appear to
be farther away.
The arrangement
of the buildings is
interesting, and
worthy of consider-
ation.   The two
roads intersect in
the middle of the
village, one of them
coming forward to
a level crossing.
The road junction
is dominated by an

DOTTED LINES SHOW APPROX
POSITION OF REAR EDGE OF
BASEBOARD, AT TRACK LEVEL,
AND OF THE PART OF RIVER
NOT VISIBLE IN DRAWING.

Fig. 28

inn, with its yard and outbuildings, and from this point the secondary
road swings to the left past a cottage and the church into the background wall.   The church, being a relatively high building, serves
the same purpose as the projecting spur of the hills in Figs. 27 and 28,
and the fringe of trees in the pair of photographs on page 83.   It
more or less effectively conceals the point where the road ends in the
background wall.   Reference to section BB shows that the ground
level is rising slightly towards the background. This is appropriate
since the view is bounded by hills, and it serves the useful purpose
of elevating the church to a slightly higher level than the foreground
buildings, to dominate the scene and provide a focal point for the
village.   Apart from the aesthetic consideration, with which we are
primarily concerned, that is, of course, exactly what the church
does in thousands of villages.

A type of country church has been represented here which has a low weatherboarded bell tower, with or without spire. The tower is often painted white, and by a process of weathering has be-

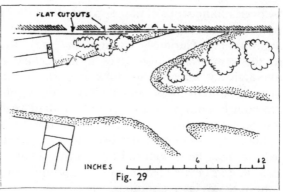

Fig. 29

come a delicate and silvery light grey. The spire, or low hipped roof, may be shingled. The main roof of such churches is often covered with red or brownish tiles. This is a better type of church for modelling purposes than the rather characterless structures with stone tower and slated spire which modellers so often contrive to produce, and photographs which have occasionally appeared in model railway journals leave the impression that many people are only aware of the existence of one kind of church : the mid-Victorian sham-Gothic. The writer has treated the subject of buildings in another book* so that detailed discussion would be out of place here, but since no drawings of churches were given in the earlier work it may not be altogether inappropriate to include a sketch, Fig. 31, of a church of the general type suggested. The one illustrated was found in Hampshire, but is typical of many parts of the country. A low spire can be added if desired, as in Fig. 30. The shingled spire, or low hipped roof, can be represented

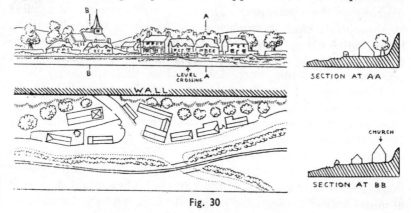

Fig. 30

*"Miniature Building Construction," Percival Marshall & Co. Ltd., 10s. 6d.

by overlapping strips of paper, painted a dark brown to which some grey has been added.   For the walls Merco old stone paper is appropriate.   Curiously enough, the grey weathered tile paper in the same series also gives a satisfactory impression of stone, although not intended for that purpose.   In many cases the nave of such churches was built in Saxon times, and may antedate the Norman Conquest by a couple of hundred years.   The other parts are usually additions made in later times.   This is not without importance to the modeller because it means that while " Gothic " features may be introduced freely in the chancel, aisles, porch, etc., they should be avoided in any part of the nave which has not been concealed by later additions.

Here is a useful hint concerning the use of stone paper for much-weathered walls.   The writer places the paper, face up, on a sheet of the coarsest sandpaper available. He then works with considerable force all over the surface

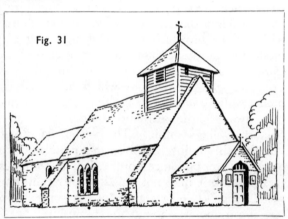

Fig. 31

with a piece of ink- or typewriter-eraser.   The result is to break the mechanical surface, and to emboss the paper with the surface structure of the sandpaper.   The same treatment can be applied in appropriate cases to brick and tile papers as well.   It will be found that building papers photograph very much better when so treated because they have an actual texture instead of just a printed representation of one.

Returning to Fig. 30, consideration of the stables behind the inn, and also of the church, will suggest that there is some compression or foreshortening in the middle distance ; the stables in fact are almost touching the steep hillside and the church is separated from it by a space of barely 3 in.   This is just enough room to allow the introduction of one or two trees which are high enough to be seen above the roof of the church.   They establish a kind of visual barrier between the middle distance, and the far distance and help to create an illusion that there is more space than actually exists. It will help the illusion if lighter and colder tones are used for the hillside to throw it back by contrast with the stronger and richer tones of the foreground in the manner we have already considered in this chapter.

The principle of employing lighter tones in the background can be applied to buildings as well as to natural scenery. Printed building papers can be made lighter in tone in two ways : they can be worked up with white or light-toned poster colours. When using brick papers the darker toned bricks can be picked out with a small pointed brush charged with a lighter colour or a thin transparent wash can in some cases be applied all over the paper. The other method is to work over the paper—before it is cut up and used —with a hard rubber. This has the effect of removing some of the ink so that if carried far enough the paper begins to show through. The best way is to combine these two methods, and as a matter of fact building papers should always be treated with hard rubber or pumice powder when paint is to be applied in order to give them a tooth.

When experience has been gained the worker may feel inclined to proceed a step further by modelling distant buildings to a slightly smaller scale than that employed in the foreground. The same brick and tile papers can be used provided that the change of scale is not too pronounced, but it is advisable to work up the papers a little, as described in the last paragraph, so that brick and tile courses shall not be too obvious. The worker who is sufficiently skilled can dispense with building papers and substitute washes of appropriate colour for background buildings. If the scale of the railway is 4 mm. to 1 ft., which is roughly $\frac{3}{16}$ in. to 1 ft., the scale used for background buildings might be $\frac{1}{8}$ in. to 1 ft. but for all ordinary purposes it is not advisable to go further than that, at least until considerable skill has been acquired.

In Fig. 32 a farm is represented. It is separated from the railway, which is on a lower level, by a cutting. Note that the buildings are disposed at slightly different angles to produce a natural and informal effect. The ground to the left of the farmhouse, behind the bridge, could be worked up as ploughed land with furrows, while on the hillside to the right the possibility of grazing cattle is suggested. For this purpose the plastic farm animals supplied by G. N. Slater are the most suitable. There are also sets of lead animals which can be obtained at toyshops and some

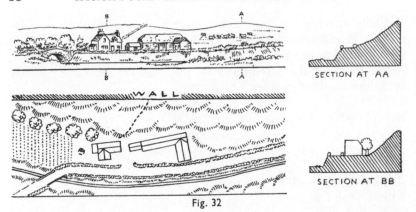

SECTION AT AA

SECTION AT BB

Fig. 32

small stationers. These must be repainted with matt colours to get rid of the shine, but being slightly overscale, are really only suitable for use in the foreground. The farmyard should be provided with such details as a dog kennel and horse trough. A plough and a tractor are easily modelled and help to infuse life into the picture. One of the older tractors, painted light blue with bright red wheels, provides a very welcome note of colour against the more sober tones of buildings.

A dry-stone wall, dividing two fields, meanders over the hill into the distance behind the farmhouse. It can be made of old stone paper stuck round a strip of thick card which has been partly cut through where necessary to enable it to bend sufficiently to follow the irregularities of the ground (Fig. 33). To help the effect of diminishing perspective, it can be made slightly lower at the more distant end where it dips at the horizon. It could diminish in height from, say $\frac{3}{8}$ in. to about $\frac{1}{4}$ in. In the distance the writer would apply a thin wash of poster white tinted with vandyke brown to soften and partly obliterate the pattern of the stone. Such details become imperceptible at a little distance. It may be mentioned here that the colour of Merco old stone paper can be reproduced exactly with vandyke brown and white, a fact which is occasionally very useful.

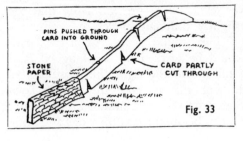

PINS PUSHED THROUGH CARD INTO GROUND

STONE PAPER

CARD PARTLY CUT THROUGH

Fig. 33

In Fig. 34 something more ambitious is suggested. The idea is a railway following a

winding course along a shelf in a deep river gorge, with a background formed by steep wooded mountain slopes with patches of
exposed rock and scree. There is a mountain torrent with a waterfall, which the railway crosses on a bridge. To the left we have an
attractive scenic feature which is seldom modelled, a concrete
avalanche gallery. It should, if space permits, be longer than the
one suggested in the drawing. The slopes directly above it should
be bare of vegetation, except for a few quick-growing mosses. Scree,
represented by fine gravel or certain kinds of " OO " gauge ballast,
should spread down the mountain side and spill over on to the roof
of the gallery as evidence of past avalanches. A few larger stones,
representing boulders can be mixed with the scree. All this should
be set in a bed of Casco glue or in a foundation of Alabastine or
some similar earth-mix. More gravel and small boulders should
be arranged below the railway along the bank of the river, and some
of the stones may be arranged to appear as if partly submerged in
the water. It may be added that avalanche galleries are not
confined to countries overseas; there are several examples to be
found within the British Isles.

For such a setting as is suggested here the trees might be pines,
if the worker feels equal to representing individual species. It
may be noted that two lines of railway could pursue roughly parallel
courses on opposite banks of the river, one raised up on a rock shelf
as shown in the drawing, the other down in the valley, and only a
few feet above water level. To introduce variety, one of them could
run partly in a tunnel. An attractive alternative would be a
gravelled road following the windings of the river.

A ground plan has not been prepared, as in the foregoing
examples, nor has the idea been fully developed for any particular
scale, but a couple of sections have been included, one of them
through the avalanche gallery, which should convey a general idea
of the space required for a satisfactory effect in " OO " gauge. It
is open to question whether such an ambitious project could be
carried out altogether satisfactorily on a baseboard only 2 ft. wide,
even with single track. A baseboard 3 ft. wide has been assumed,
which is sufficient to allow reasonable scope. If the baseboard
width must be restricted to 2 ft. it might be better to employ
practically vertical cliffs behind the railway, rather than a slope.
This would, of course, demand some change in the scenic treatment
since only in very exceptional circumstances can a tree contrive
to grow out of a cliff face. Still, a few tress could be worked in here

Fig. 34

and there on ledges to relieve the bareness of the rock face, and the worker can plant as many as he likes at the top of the cliff where they will break up the skyline. A suggestion for treatment on these lines is given in Fig. 35.

A minimum useful length of baseboard for scenery of the kind shown in Figs. 34 and 35 might be estimated at about 9 ft. for " OO " gauge : one of the walls of a small room, say. Most of us can spare that much space for a really attractive piece of scenic work. It is hardly necessary to say that the mountains should not terminate too abruptly where we approach the plains, but should diminish in height as progressively as space considerations may permit.

In Fig. 34 there are about 28 trees, not an outrageous demand if mass-production methods are used as advocated in the preceding chapter. Those which are well in the background, and partly concealed, need not be so well shaped or so well finished as those in more prominent positions.

The river need not have a width of more than about 4 in. in 4 mm. scale. This is equivalent to about 25 ft. and is sufficient for a fast mountain torrent. There is, of course, no doubt that some flat painted scenery could be used to good effect, especially in the gorge above the waterfall, but we are concerned for the moment to show that it is possible, if we wish, to get along quite well without it.

Fig. 36 illustrates a type of scenic modelling which can be very effective, and which is well adapted to situations where space is restricted. This is the village or town built on a hillside, where houses or cottages rise in tiers, one above another. It enables the builder to introduce more scenic modelling and to produce a more effective massing than is possible on a flat surface. The photographic possibilities of a well designed scene of this kind are sufficiently obvious. There are many villages to be found which conform more or less to this style. As a matter of fact the drawing was suggested in the first instance by an old photograph of Staithes, in Yorkshire, although practically nothing of the original remains. A photograph of Lynmouth, in Devon, might have led to an almost identical

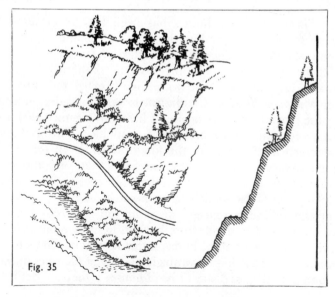

Fig. 35

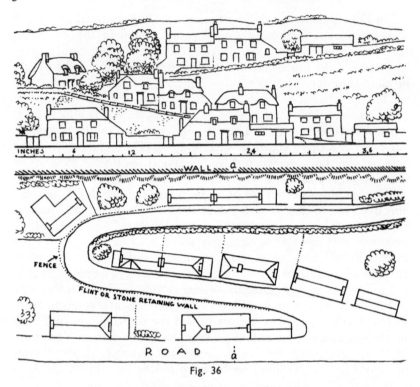

Fig. 36

result. The style of the houses has been left rather nondescript
with the idea that any reader who may feel inclined to follow the
suggestion should introduce the characteristic features of the district
in which he is interested. In any case, this is hardly the place to
discuss building details ; the writer has treated the subject very
fully in *Miniature Building Construction* to which readers may refer.

For the purpose of this drawing it has been assumed that a space
just over 3 ft. long by 19 in. deep is available. This includes the
area occupied by the road in the foreground. Even this could no
doubt be reduced somewhat by careful setting out and a more
deliberate application of foreshortened perspective. Examination
of the plan, and of the section at *aa* included in Fig. 37, shows that
most of the buildings, except those in the foreground row, are
slightly compressed in depth from back to front to economise space.
We have already given some hints on this subject in connection with
distant hills. Note the highly strategic placing of the trees in relation
to the highest and most distant row of houses ; they are deliberately

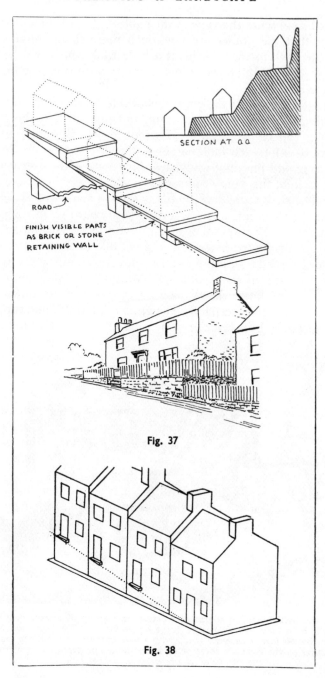

SECTION AT Q.Q

ROAD

FINISH VISIBLE PARTS
AS BRICK OR STONE
RETAINING WALL

Fig. 37

Fig. 38

arranged to obscure the view of the gable ends and thereby conceal the fact that the houses are not much more than frontages with very little back to them. This is a little trick which will be found useful in many situations where there is insufficient room for a complete building.

Fig. 37 shows what the writer believes to be the simplest method of building a row of houses on a hill, and suggests how the gardens and bases can be arranged on different levels. Start by cutting a separate base for each building, or group of buildings on the same level, using odd pieces of wallboard, plywood, or thick strawboard. Mount each of these on wood supports which have been screwed to the baseboard, or to the substructure if there is no all-over baseboard. The road is then cut, in some form of wallboard or in thick card, to conform to the disposition of the house plots, and mounted on supports of graduated height. It is advisable to arrive at the exact shape for the road by a process of trial and error, cutting the material a trifle oversize to start with and cutting bits away until it fits in nicely. The lower sketch shows a common arrangement when houses are built on a steep hill. The ground is levelled and supported where necessary by a brick or stone retaining wall. This necessarily

In the background, in course of erection, is a group of terrace houses and shops built by the method suggested in Fig. 38. The two cottages on the left form a separate group with a base of their own, but the four houses on the right are constructed as one unit, and stepped to conform to the inclination of a roadway on a steep hill.

The group of buildings shown in the last photograph after completion.

tapers in height. It simply means that the triangular gaps which must occur between the horizontal house bases and the sloping road surface are filled with pieces of card which are covered with brick or stone paper. Alternatively, they can be fixed at an angle and worked up as grass banks if the style of the buildings admits of such treatment.

It is not difficult to construct a village on several levels if the job is approached in the manner suggested above : by installing baseboards for the buildings first and then working in the roads, and other ground surfaces, to connect them. If the reader attempts to work the other way round, building a hillside first and then trying to construct houses with irregular bases to fit it he is likely to get into serious difficulties.

A rather different method may be justified in cases where several buildings are joined together in terrace form. Here it may be more convenient to treat the group as a single building and to erect it on one base. The buildings on the higher levels have what we may term extended " foundations " to elevate them to the required height.

The idea will be more readily understood by reference to Fig. 38. Needless to say such details as doorsteps should be fitted after the roadway is in place.

TREATMENT OF CORNERS

If one were fortunate enough to be building a room especially for model railway purposes one would ask the builder to carry the plaster round the corners in a curve with a radius of about 18 in. or rather more. One would thus avoid definite corners and escape from those irritating vertical lines on the sky which detract from the effect of so many model railway photographs. Naturally there are very few cases indeed in which this is possible, but when a room has been allocated permanently to model railway purposes it is quite practicable, and not difficult to form a sky background of thin pulp board or lino and to carry it round the corners in a gentle curve. Wood supports could be fixed to the wall behind to provide rigidity. This is illustrated in Fig. 39. The curved board can start 2 in. or 3 in. below the minimum baseboard level and continue up to the picture rail, or as high as the *width* of the material may permit. The subject of sky backgrounds is treated in more detail in a later chapter.

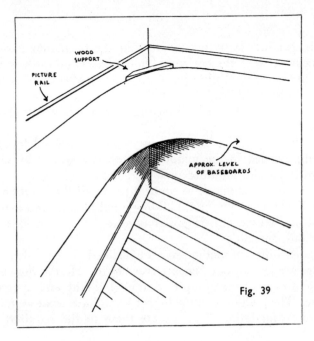

Fig. 39

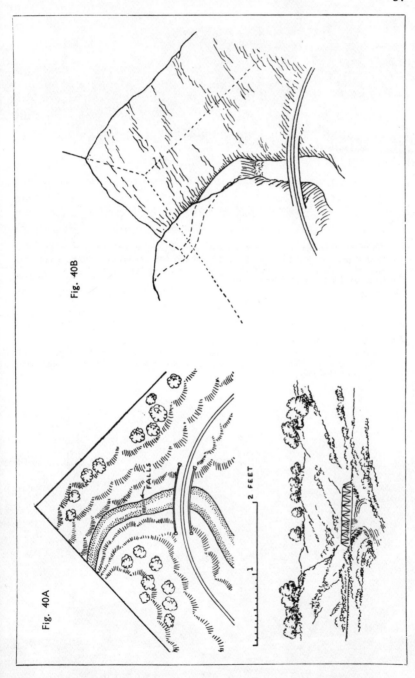

Fig. 40B

Fig. 40A

FALLS

2 FEET

1

An interesting example of corner treatment—a small sawmill and timber concern with a private siding which approaches the premises through the gate seen on the left. The precise position of the corner of the room is just apparent from evidence to be found in the sky !

Another example of corner treatment ; a quarry with screening plant and light railway. In this case also the reader will not be in doubt as to where the corner of the room is located.

But we must assume that in most cases it is not practicable to do anything to conceal the corners, and that the worker must just make the best of them. Something can be done to mask corner, however, by erecting church spires, factory chimneys, and high hills, in suitable situations.

Corners do at least provide convenient sites for scenic features, however, and in cases where the baseboards may have to be rather narrow, and space is generally restricted, they may be the only places where anything ambitious can be undertaken. They offer suitable sites for factories, quarries, and the like, where railway sidings can be located. And in addition to such industrial uses features such as farms, villages, and river gorges framed between steep hills, at once suggest themselves. Fig. 40A is a suggestion for a scene of the last-named description. It is planned for 4 mm. scale and the radius of the railway curve is about 2 ft. If space permits it would, perhaps, be preferable for the bridge to be built straight, although there are plenty of curved railway bridges to be found.

It will be found that a waterfall can be included with very satisfactory effect in this little scene ; its position is indicated. The river is made to wind so that at the point where it meets the wall it is more or less effectively hidden by the steep mountain slopes. This will be clear from Fig. 40B. The style of scenic treatment can be similar to that shown in Fig. 34 and a corner of this kind could form part of a scene of that description.

Fig. 41 is the plan of a farm as executed by the writer. Note that the farmyard is raised about 2 in. above the road and railway. The ground is supposed to have been excavated for the road and by raising the farm we obtain a bolder effect than would be possible if everything were on one level. The baseboard of the farmyard is a piece of ½ in. soft pulp board, supported on wood blocks to bring it to the required height. The pond was cut out of the pulp board with a keyhole saw, held at an angle to produce the effect of sloping banks. A piece of stiff white card was glued and pinned to the underside of the hole thus formed and treated with distemper and then with cellophane to represent water. A few patches of green sawdust, laid on Durofix, give the effect of weeds floating on the surface and some sand was added in a few places close to the banks. The banks of the pond were painted with brown poster colour and sprinkled patchily with sawdust and sand and a few bushes added.

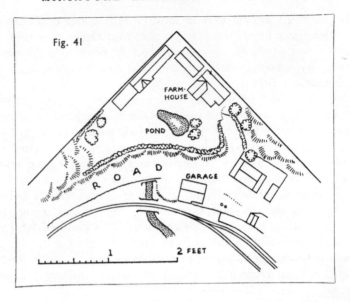

Fig. 41

The surface of the farmyard was painted with light yellowish-brown paint and treated with gum and sawdust. Drawings for the farmhouse and buildings will be found in *Miniature Building Construction*. There is a section of painted back scene in the space on the left, between the farm buildings and the rising slope, which provides a glimpse of standing corn. Any deficiencies in the execution of this are discreetly masked by the two trees and a hedge. Hence only a glimpse of the distant view is obtained, which is the best way to use flat scenery unless the worker happens to be very skilful at such work. Nevertheless the painted background serves its purpose in that it suggests that the distance *is there*, and that the farm consists of something more than just a farmyard. The result is shown in the photograph on page 101.

Another suggestion to occupy a space of similar dimensions is illustrated in Fig. 42. This is a village street, enclosed between hills. In this example, as in the last, the ground level has been raised above that of the railway, and the latter runs in a cutting which is spanned by a road bridge. The church has been located so that its spire may to some extent mask the corner of the room, although it must be admitted that whether this little subterfuge is really worth bothering about is open to question. A cart track leads up rather steeply to an isolated house or farm on the downs to the left.

The farm shown in plan in Fig. 41

It may be as well to utter a word of warning here concerning the scenic treatment of corners. The worker will very soon discover that when the baseboards are more than about 2 ft. 6 in. wide it becomes next to impossible to execute fine work in the extreme corner of the room. The task is so exhausting and back-breaking that few people could continue at it for very long. The reason for this may not be immediately obvious for most people can reach across a baseboard 2 ft. 6 in. or 3 ft. wide without excessive discomfort. This overlooks the fact, however, that in the corner we are dealing with a diagonal, and that if the baseboards are 2 ft. 6 in. wide the distance from the nearest point of the free operating area to the extreme corner is about 3 ft. 5 in. If the baseboards are 3 ft. wide the distance will be about 4 ft. 3 in. which is more than anyone can manage without an extreme effort. For this reason it is advisable to build corner sets on portable sub-baseboards, which can be constructed and finished off in comfort on the workbench—where they can be turned around and worked on from whatever angle may be most convenient. They should only be fixed in place on the main baseboard when complete. Any work which may be necessary to

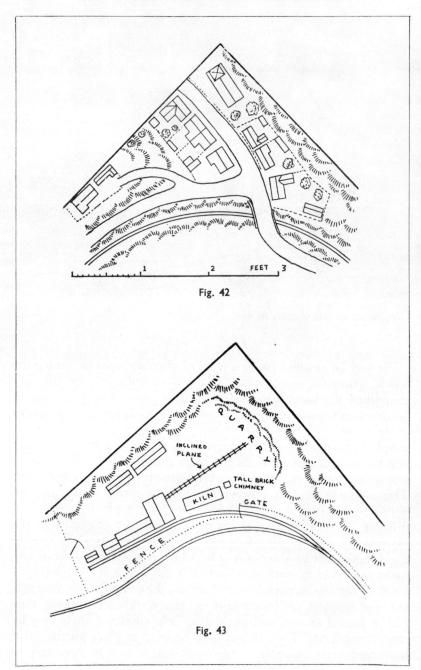

Fig. 42

Fig. 43

A village scene with simple built-up hillside background which avoids the use of flat backdrops.

blend them into the surroundings can then be undertaken, and as this will apply mostly to the foreground edge it will not present any back-breaking problems. Such sub-baseboards can be pieces of wallboard cut to the required triangular shape, or even in certain cases a piece of stiff strawboard. It should not require much rein-forcing or bracing because once it is in position on the baseboard or substructure it can be secured with a few nails or screws and will not thereafter be subject to any stresses.

Fig. 43 is a suggestion for the arrangement of a brickyard or quarry. The layout, and the style of the buildings, can be much the same for either, but for a quarry the brick kiln would, of course, be omitted. The drawing shows a short inclined plane by means of which narrow-gauge hopper wagons are drawn up out of the quarry by a winding engine. In a particular brick field which the writer has in mind the material quarried was limestone. The colour as seen in the open workings may be represented by gamboge. It is not advisable to use the colour alone, however ; a more realistic result will be obtained if traces of other colours, such as black, white, and brown, are worked in at random.

CHAPTER SEVEN

The Sky Background and Lighting

IT is apparent that for scenic modelling to be displayed effectively some form of light sky-blue background must be provided. If, for any reason, this is out of the question the next best is for the walls to be distempered a plain cream. Any form of patterned wall-paper is about the worst thing which can be imagined ; it renders decent photography impossible and completely spoils the effect of any kind of scenic modelling. If the worker is at liberty to take such measures as he may think fit the simplest way is to distemper the walls of the room a light sky-blue up to the picture rail level. I say advisedly a *light* sky-blue because blue distempers as sold are usually rather darker in tone than is necessary or desirable. The effect of a blue room is usually rather sombre and for this reason one can very well mix the distemper with an equal quantity of white. The effect will be much more cheerful and less likely to clash with other colours. It is not necessary to paint the woodwork to match the walls ; blue goes very well with a colour such as light cream or buff. If you are painting the woodwork, don't fall into the trap of using a darker shade of blue for the result would probably be most unpleasant. The best colour of all for doors and window frames would, perhaps, be a light dove grey.

In some cases, of course, it is not practicable to treat the walls of the room, and the best alternative is to hang lengths of linoleum or thin board, such as ¼ in. Essex board, which have been treated with blue distemper. Any lino can be used in this way ; even a patterned one can be effectively covered with two, or at most three, coats. It is important that it should be thoroughly clean before distemper is applied. Give it a wash with soda or Manger's sugar soap. Essex board is capable of giving a particularly fresh and brilliant sky effect if the distemper is applied direct to the natural surface. No size should be applied or other preliminary treatment used. The porous surface will take up a lot of distemper, but it will spread very evenly and cleanly.

The sheets of pulp board or lino can be secured to the wall with small nails, panel pins, or screws in Rawlplugs. The top edge should be as high as the width of the material permits, allowing the lower edge to hang down 2 in. below the baseboards. In cases where it is not considered permissible to deface the walls, or if they are too hard to take nails conveniently, a very simple alternative is available : lengths of 2 in. by 1 in batten, or a simple architrave moulding, can be nailed to the upper edges of the sheets of board or lino. They are then hung from the picture rail with ordinary picture hangers and lengths of wire or chain as in Fig. 44. It is, of course, true that it will be difficult to conceal the joins between sections of sky background entirely, but if the walls must not be painted or defaced this is undoubtedly the best alternative which can be devised.

Another possibility is to use plain sky-blue wallpaper and to apply it horizontally to the walls, either with paste or with pins. The latter alternative is hardly to be recommended as the paper is liable to drag into creases and to tear away from the pins in course of time. If pins must be used, it is suggested that a strip of paper, about 3 in. or 4 in. wide, should be pasted to the back surface along the top edge. This will make the material firmer and provide a better hold for the pins.

Being quite light in weight, wallpaper could be attached to a wall by running a strip of masking tape along the top edge, allowing the lower edge to hang free. This might not last indefinitely, but would serve well as a more or less temporary expedient. It may be noted that by this method the paper could be hung without damage to the walls since the masking tape could be pulled away quite cleanly when required.

A few workers have installed a sky of a type which may be likened to the cycloramas used in many theatres. The idea is illustrated in Fig. 45. Thin composition or plywood boards are bent to a quarter-cylindrical form and mounted on a wood framework so that the top edge is brought forward approximately level with the front edge of the baseboard. A pelmet board is usually fixed to the front edge and serves to conceal electric light fittings spaced at convenient intervals to provide reasonably even illumination.

By this method the upper edge of the sky is concealed from view and something of the effect of a stage is obtained. At least the concealed lamps offer the advantage of complete freedom from glare. This method is very suitable for public exhibitions, but the writer is of the opinion that such ponderous and elaborate arrangements might be rather disconcerting, or even repellant, in an ordinary room of normal dimensions. The difficulties which will be encountered at the corners of the room, and where doors intervene, need hardly be stressed. It may be added that such fittings might prove something of a nuisance when photography was being undertaken. It is not to be supposed that the fixed lights behind the pelmet boards would provide much scope for effect and movable photographic lamps would be required in the normal manner. It is practically certain that the fixed pelmet boards would seriously restrict the placing of the lamps by throwing shadows just where they were least wanted.

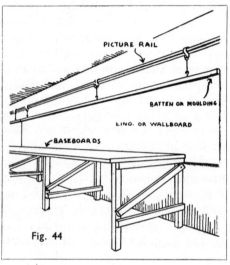

Fig. 44

A far more important matter is the provision of really adequate lighting in the railway room, and in this respect it must be admitted that most model railways fail lamentably. A model railway undoubtedly needs to be better illuminated than an ordinary living room of the same area. Even in quite a small room a single powerful bulb suspended in the centre is far from ideal because even if it should provide adequate illumination the worker finds that his own shadow is constantly getting in his way whenever he attempts to do anything on the baseboards. This is quite bad enough when operating the railway, but when construction or maintenance work is undertaken the only escape from what rapidly becomes an infuriating nuisance is to provide a portable lamp on a long flex which can be placed anywhere in the room.

The best method is to have a number of lamps of rather low power (say 60 watts) located at short intervals over the railway.

They may be at a height of about 5 ft. above the baseboards, and should, if possible, be spaced not more than 4 ft. apart. It is absolutely essential to the comfort of those using the room that they should be adequately shaded. There are many ways of arranging a lighting system of this kind, and that shown in Fig. 46 is as simple

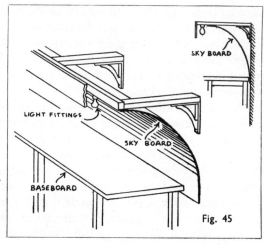

Fig. 45

as any. A long batten, which may be the ordinary 2 in. by 1 in. material, is supported by large shelf brackets which are Rawl-plugged to the wall. Shorter lengths of batten form extensions to the brackets with the object of bringing the lamps forward about 2 ft. or 3 ft., the exact distance being governed by the width of the baseboards. For a wall 8 ft. to 10 ft. long a 6 ft. length of batten would suffice, and, being quite light in weight, it could be supported securely on two brackets. For longer walls one or more additional supports would be advisable. The lamp fittings are ordinary batten holders and the shades could be made of plywood or sheet metal. It will be seen that they are closed on three sides and open on the fourth which faces towards the wall. The wiring could be carried out with ordinary rubber - covered cable, carried along the upper surfaces of the battens under clips, and brought to a 5 amp, 2-pin, socket

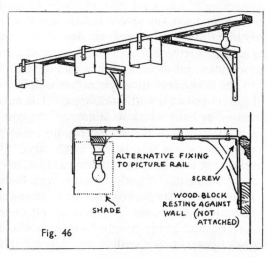

Fig. 46

at one end. The current supply could be taken to the fitting by ordinary flex and a plug. Such a semi-temporary arrangement has the advantage that if alterations are being made to the railway which necessitate any change in the lighting it can be shifted, removed temporarily, or modified, without having to interfere with permanent wiring.

A slight modification is shown in the lower diagram, Fig. 46, which may prove very convenient when a picture rail is available for the fittings. It will be seen that the diagram gives what is in effect a sectional view of the arrangement. The shelf brackets are attached to the wall at one point only : by a woodscrew into the picture rail. The lower end of the bracket hangs free, but a small block of wood of the same thickness as the picture rail is attached to it so that it hangs vertical. It will be seen that with this method there is no need to plug the wall. The screw holes in the picture rail are very easily made good with plastic wood, or any wood filler, if it is desired to remove the fittings at any time.

As an alternative, the lamp batten could be suspended by chains from hooks fixed into the ceiling joists if this method should be more convenient. It may be pointed out that the cost of a lighting installation of this kind would be very low indeed ; hardly anything is required beyond a few feet of batten, some shelf brackets, the lampholders, and wire. The lampshades, presumably, would be fabricated from any material which was available. It is really infinitely more satisfactory to set to work systematically and arrange something of this kind than to fiddle about rigging up lamps in odd corners and festooning the ceiling and the walls with rather inconsequent bits and pieces of flex and two-way adaptors. Such arrangements produce an untidy atmosphere which it is not good to work in and worse to bring visitors into.

The fluorescent tube system has a lot in its favour for the lighting of model railways and workshops. The tubes supply a practically shadowless light over a wide area. The cost of installation is rather high, but, candle power for candle power, can be offset by the saving in the consumption of electricity. The slightly cold colour of the light is rather disconcerting at first, but the writer's experience suggests that one quickly becomes accustomed to it. It is as well to remember that fluorescent light, having a different spectrum to half-watt light, might produce an effect on the colours of model scenery which could hardly be estimated in advance. Fluorescent light appears to the writer to be less suitable for use with lathes or other revolving machinery because stroboscopic effects are liable to be more pronounced than with half-watt light from an alternating current source.

CHAPTER EIGHT

Flat Scenic Backgrounds

THIS is not an easy chapter to write, if it is to serve a useful purpose, for it is one thing to describe the building of scenery in three-dimensional solid form, and quite another to help readers to achieve a representation on a flat surface after the manner of the artist. Such work cannot be undertaken with much prospect of success unless the technique of representing distance and perspective, light and shade, has been acquired at least to a small extent. Nevertheless, it is surprising what untrained people can accomplish if they are prepared to approach the subject in a systematic way, and to confine themselves to a limited range of easily secured effects.

It is realised that many people will not feel inclined to undertake the task of painting their own scenery and probably the most popular alternative is to utilise and adapt large railway and other posters. The usual method is to remove the sky, by cutting along the skyline, and to paste or pin the remaining part to a skyblue background. The joints between one poster and the next are usually concealed, as far as possible, by high foreground features such as hills and high buildings, modelled in three dimensions. This method has produced excellent results in the hands of a few workers, but the difficulties are considerable nevertheless. It may be difficult to find posters which accord sufficiently well with the modeller's idea of what the scenic setting should be, and in which the detail is the right size to accord with the scale of the foreground. The scale to which objects in the poster are drawn should, if anything, be smaller than that of the railway and of solid objects in the foreground, whereas it will be found that most posters suggest a larger scale than 4 mm. to the foot, but might be used successfully with a " O " gauge railway. But this is not all : these railway posters are produced by first class artists who have strongly in-dividualised styles, and any two of them will be found to differ considerably in the amount and type of detail they present, in their selection and use of colour and wash, and in their handling of light and atmospheric effect. One secures his effect by a bold use of distant blues and purples while another relies on foreground greens and browns. It follows that to select a number of posters by different hands which can be used in juxtaposition without marked differences of treatment becoming evident would be very difficult.

And there is a further objection to posters in that they are intended for display ; *they are designed to compete with their surroundings*, to catch the eye and create a definite impression by virtue of their merits. Now that is exactly what we do not want in a model railway background, which should simply round off the foreground picture and refrain from calling undue attention to itself. A good poster may overwhelm the foreground and compete for attention with the railway itself. The colours, intended to be seen in the open air and in competition with all the colour and movement of a street or station approach, may be too bold to accord with the atmosphere of a model railway room of normal dimensions, and there may be some difficulty in making the colours of the modelled foreground harmonise with those of the poster.

For these reasons specially painted scenery seems preferable if the reader feels disposed to tackle the subject ; it can at least be designed to fit the site and unnecessarily bold effects can be avoided. But it may be mentioned here that if the reader has considered the general implication of the preceding chapters he may have formed the opinion that by the consistent use of modelled hills and grass banks, and the like, it is possible to dispense with a flat painted background entirely. This is perfectly true, and it may provide the best solution for those who lack the time or the inclination to experiment. As a matter of fact the writer's Madder Valley Railway was designed almost entirely on that principle in its original form. Only after several years, and as a result of gradual changes in the layout and setting, did the writer begin to experiment with sections of painted scenery. It will be found, however, that there are usually odd corners which it is difficult to finish off satis-factorily by the former method, and it was this consideration which first led the writer to try his hand at scene painting. A typical case is the road leading " off stage " into the distance through a break in a line of hills.   In such cases, if the area to be covered is relatively small, it may be that a section cut from a poster, or from a coloured picture, may be worked in quite successfully.   Usually in these circumstances the background picture can be enclosed on both sides by hill slopes so that we obtain what may be termed a peepshow view which appears satisfactory, because it can be pushed into the background by the setting which frames it.   Fig. 47 will

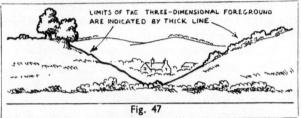

LIMITS OF THE THREE-DIMENSIONAL FOREGROUND ARE INDICATED BY THICK LINE

Fig. 47

help to explain the   principle. Even so, many readers will probably think it better to produce the scene themselves, using as the basis some picture found in a book or illustrated magazine and modifying the scale, detail, and colour, etc.

It seems then that the best which can be attempted in the space at the writer's disposal is to endeavour to show the reader how he can produce one or two simple, and generally useful, effects, such as a tree skyline, and a view of distant rolling downs, which will serve to round off the much more important foreground work, and from which the reader may hope to produce more interesting variations when some experience has been gained.

We may first consider the form which the writer's own scenic efforts take, and it must be made clear before we go further, that there is more than one method of obtaining the desired result. Some people use oil paint, for example ; whereas the writer has always favoured poster colours.   Oils may be more satisfactory, and even easier to manage, in the hands of an experienced worker, but it is probable that the beginner will be less intimidated by poster colours, and this is, in any case, nothing more than an account of the writer's own methods.   The writer's scenery is painted on thick white card after the design has been sketched in pencil and cut along the skyline.   Sometimes scissors are used and sometimes a razor blade for corners which are difficult to reach with scissors.   Alternatively thin wallboard can be used, but must be cut with a keyhole saw or fretsaw.   The edge should be rounded off slightly with sandpaper which will give an effect of depth to the outlines of trees and distant hills.   This backdrop, of card, or wallboard, is painted and mounted against a sky background, produced by one of the methods described in the preceding chapter. The backdrop is prepared in sections, as long as may be considered convenient for handling, and several pieces of card may be glued together with an overlap of several inches, up to a maximum of about 6 ft. Anything longer than this is too liable to sag and get damaged while being handled. The overlaps between adjacent sections of card are arranged to dip down behind the solid foreground work as shown in Fig. 48. In this sketch the outline of the card is indicated by a thick continuous line and the glued overlap of several inches will be noted. The upper edge of the solid foreground work is shown by a broken line. In some cases features such as groups of trees or buildings can be used to mask the joins between sections. These can be painted on separate pieces of card or paper and stuck in place. Cutout backgrounds, such as we are considering, are usually intended to stand behind solid hills or railway embankments or to be glimpsed intermittently between trees and modelled buildings, and the more emphasis one can place on the foreground (and the less on the background) the better. And naturally one only paints those parts of the scenic background which will be visible above the solid foreground work, allowing, of course, a safety margin of about a couple of inches. These cutout background sections are secured in position against the wall by whatever method may be most convenient ; sometimes they can be attached to the wall by two or three inconspicuous pins. Usually, however, it is better to attach lengths of stripwood to their lower edge so that they can stand on the baseboard, or substructure.

Obviously, the best thing to do is to arrange a gap of not less than an inch, and preferably 2 in. between the built-up foreground and the

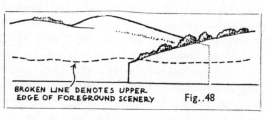

BROKEN LINE DENOTES UPPER EDGE OF FOREGROUND SCENERY   Fig. 48

wall so that the background sections can stand clear of both, as in Fig. 49, which gives a better illusion of distance. It may be mentioned that if the background sections are very close to the wall, trouble will be encountered when taking photographs through the edge of the background throwing shadows on the sky. If a gap of about 1 in. or more can be allowed there is a much

better chance of manipulating the lamps so that inconvenient
shadows drop down behind the background cutout where they are
out of sight of the camera.

If the backdrops could be made and arranged in position before
the foreground was built up the question of mounting them on the
baseboards would be simpler than it is ; they could be secured
permanently with wood blocks or brackets and screws.   In practice,
however, this sequence would not appeal to many people ; it
seems that the foreground must be made first, and the flat background then made to conform to it, and to most workers it would
appear all wrong to work the other way round.   The normal
sequence is obviously to build the railway and its more immediate
surroundings first, and
only after a lapse of time,
months or even years per-
haps, to consider com-
pleting the scenic picture.

It has probably oc-
curred to the reader that
the backdrops could be
painted on artists' water
colour paper and pasted
to the sky-blue back-
ground. There is nothing
against this proceeding
except that most of us
may feel rather reluctant

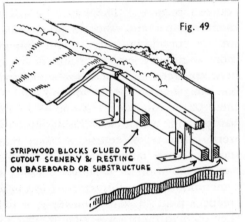

Fig. 49

STRIPWOOD BLOCKS GLUED TO
CUTOUT SCENERY & RESTING
ON BASEBOARD OR SUBSTRUCTURE

to stick anything to our nice blue background, especially if it happens
to be the wall of the room.   And if after a time, the worker becomes
dissatisfied with his first attempts and wishes to replace them with
new ones, the chances are that it will be impossible to remove them
without damage to the sky, which will probably need re-distemper-
ing afterwards.   There is also the consideration that the ability
to shift the backdrops a few inches to the right or to the left, or
even to change them about, may make a surprising and gratifying
difference to the effect.

Another point which must be considered is the height of the
backgrounds ; in other words, what should be the average height
in inches of the " skyline " above the general level of the railway
baseboards ? I do not think that any definite rule can be formu-
lated, but my own conclusion is that for a 4 mm. scale railway a

height of about 8 in. or at most 9 in. is quite enough. For mountains this can of course be increased to whatever the reader likes within reason. This refers, of course, exclusively to flat scenery ; there need be no definite restrictions on the height of hills and cliffs which are modelled in the round. These are near to the observer, and solid, so that the delicate questions of perspective which affect flat scenery do not arise. If this should appear a little paradoxical, it is only necessary to point out that quite a small hill, viewed from a distance of a few hundred yards, may appear to rise higher in the sky than the Alps or the Pyrenees many miles away.

Some writers have maintained, more particularly in American modelling journals, that the skyline should be located at the eye level of a person of average height : that is to say about 5 ft. 3 in. above the floor of the room. This, it is claimed, should be maintained quite irrespective of what the height of the railway baseboards may happen to be. Thus if the baseboards are, say, 3 ft. above the floor the skyline would be about 2 ft. 3 in. above the baseboards. The contention is based on the fact that the skyline (or rather the horizon) is always at eye level, whatever the position of the observer may be, as the reader can verify by reference to any textbook on perspective. It seems impossible to refute this argument on theoretical or mathematical grounds, but there is no doubt that it does not work out in practice. It might work in cases where the view was bounded by high mountains but for any other kind of terrain you would get an impression from most viewpoints that the landscape was tipped up at an angle, something like the curious effect one observes from an aeroplane which is banking heavily. It must be allowed that the result might be satisfactory in a large hall where the spectators could stand away from the railway and view the scene from a distance of several yards, but that is impossible in an ordinary room and in any case contrary to the natural tendency of most people. I do not usually indulge in dogmatic statements, but this seems a rather special case and I feel that such a theory makes nothing but nonsense when applied to the home model railway, however it may be under the conditions of a public exhibition where the movements of spectators can be controlled by fixed barriers.

In our considerations of subjects for scenery we may start with what is probably the simplest motif for the beginner to reproduce : a tree background which completely closes off the distance as suggested in Fig. 50. The reader might think that a range of bare grass-covered downs would be easier for a first attempt but this is not necessarily true because in a scene of that type we are confronted with the problem of distant planes and aerial perspective. When the distance is revealed we necessarily have a succession of planes at progressively increasing distances from the observer and to suggest this convincingly we must make the more distant ones lighter in tone than the nearer ones. We must also give the distant planes a bluish or greyish tinge to simulate the effect produced on colours by the intervening layers of air. Unless we achieve at least partial success in this the result will be rather unreal and flat. Now in the case of the suggested tree background this difficulty does not arise because the trees are all about the same distance from the observer. Hence we can, if we wish to reduce matters to their simplest terms, represent them with two or three shades of green only, a very light one for those parts of the foliage which are assumed to receive the direct light of the sun, a darker green for the parts which are not in direct sunlight, and perhaps a still darker colour, almost black, for the deepest shadows underneath the masses of foliage. If we like we can dodge the problem of representing the trunks by arranging walls, modelled trees, and hedges, to conceal the lower parts from view. Thus we arrive at something on the lines of Fig. 50. It is not, of course, suggested that this simple scheme provides a fully developed presentation of the subject, but it may help people with little or no experience of drawing or painting, and when intelligently combined with foreground objects it will do what the average worker requires. We can elaborate the simple colour scheme suggested above if we feel inclined ; we can use different greens for different kinds of tree, with russet browns for beech and splashes of cream and yellow for the flower masses of such trees as chestnut and laburnum. And we can give the trees more definite form by allowing the trunks and boughs to appear through the foliage here and there. But here we shall deal only with what anyone should be able to accomplish if they consider it worth while to make the effort. When the worker has succeeded in producing something after the style of Fig. 50, the next step would be to go out, armed with the confidence which has been gained, make sketches from nature, attempt to jot down some notes about colour which will aid the memory, and then try to produce a rather more personal and varied version based on the same theme.

We must be quite clear about one matter ; it is essential to assume that our trees are too far away for individual leaves to be noticed. Only broad masses of foliage can be shown and if the reader once permits himself to be drawn into the trap of trying to show individual leaves, by stippling or some similar device, he will certainly get into very serious and exhausting difficulties, and the sooner he starts over again the better.

Sunlight and highlight tones have been mentioned already, and these words bring us to a subject which calls for some consideration. For our purpose it is almost essential to assume that the sun is shining because it casts shadows, and we are dependent on shadows to give things shape and roundness. The sun provides objects with a light side and a dark side. A skilled artist can, of course, produce the appearance of roundness on a dull day when there are no cast shadows, but an untrained beginner could hardly hope to do so. Hence the worker must decide before he starts in which quarter of the sky the sun is supposed to be. The writer always works on the assumption that it is on the left, as will be clear enough in Fig. 50, and puts shadows on the right side of objects, but this, of course, is purely a personal predilection and the other way round would serve just as well. It is important, however, to be consistent about it ; if we start by putting the sun on the left we should continue to do so throughout and ignore the fact that the railway curves round the walls of a room. We have to pretend that, like most full-size railways, it goes from one place to another on an approximately straight course, and if we attempted to change the angle of the assumed lighting for each wall of the room all sorts of difficulties would arise. The transition from one kind of lighting to another at the corners would be too difficult to manage.

In speaking of the sun as being on the left (or right) it should be understood that it is also assumed to be fairly high in the sky, and that the light is falling at an angle of, say, fifty or sixty degrees to horizontal. We endeavour to paint our shadows with this in mind, as far as may be practicable and necessary, but the reader need not be unduly conscientious and meticulous on the subject because only broad impressions count, and there is certainly no need to make the shadows very strong or very pronounced. So long as they are just bold enough to give the necessary impression of roundness and depth that is usually sufficient, and they will, of course, diminish in intensity as objects recede from the viewer, until in the extreme distance there is seldom any real need to indicate shadows at all ; masses of colour suggesting the outlines of trees or hills are sufficient.

Before any attempt is made to paint scenery a little preliminary practice in the use of tools and materials is advisable ; the reader is advised, if, like the writer, he uses poster colours, to experiment with the accepted watercolour method of laying on even and graduated washes of colour. That is really essential to successful results and once the art has been mastered more than half the difficulties which may have prevented the reader from trying his hand at such work before will vanish. For practice purposes it is useful to try several different kinds of card and paper, for one can hardly fail to gain confidence and experience by familiarising oneself with the idiosyncrasies of different surfaces. And the reader will thus discover which surfaces are likely to be amenable and which are not. Cartridge paper and any kind of white card which may be available can be tried, even white cardboard boxes, for although these are not likely to be useful it may be interesting to note how they react to colour. Use the colours which you expect to employ most when painting actual scenery for you will gain some preliminary experience as to how they should be diluted to produce different depths of tone.

Take the sheet of card or paper ; pin it to a drawing board (or to something which will serve as one) by the top edge. Prop the board up at an angle of about sixty degrees. Mix the poster colour in a saucer, or any shallow vessel. Dilute it with plenty of water for the first trials so as to produce quite a light tint. Moisten the surface of the card with a large brush (one about 1 in. wide for preference) and wait about a minute for the water to sink in and even itself up. Mark lightly in pencil the limits of the area you are going to cover. Start with an area about six inches square and increase this to a foot or more after two or three trials. Use a brush not less than ⅜ in. wide, but whether it is round or flat does not appear to be of much moment. Charge the brush with colour, and apply it with bold *horizontal* strokes, alternately from right to left and from left to right, *starting at the top and always working downwards*. Work fairly quickly and let the strokes overlap, but don't " go back " if you can avoid it. Remember that the board should be propped up at quite a steep angle so that the colour will run downwards and thus tend to even itself up. There is, I suppose, a certain knack in maintaining an even pressure (or, to be more explicit, an even *lack* of pressure) so that the colour flows off the brush evenly. This is one of those things which it is almost impossible to define in words but which is quickly sensed once a start has been made. If you are accustomed to the handling of ordinary decorator's oil colours you must forget all about it ;   the method is different and one does not " work " the paint to obtain an even surface as with decorator's paint. Put it on as quickly as possible and leave it alone.

The first attempt may not be very encouraging, but after a few more the reader will find that he is beginning to acquire the feel and the touch and can cover a considerable area so that when dry it is reasonably even in tone and free from pronounced patchiness. It may be suggested that the effect produced by adding a little white to colours should now be investigated, both to observe the effect on the tone and on the behaviour of the colour on the surface. It is often better to control the depth of tone by the addition of white than by dilution. Generally speaking, it imparts a greyish tinge to colours and for this reason may be useful when representing distant planes where colours are softened by what is called " aerial per-spective."

It may be hoped that even if the reader was at first disposed to resist the whole business he may find that by the time he can apply an even wash his interest will be aroused and he will be ready to go a step further. So let us return to the tree background, Fig. 50, where it will be seen that a grid of vertical and horizontal lines has been placed over the drawing. It is hardly necessary to describe how a grid of this kind is used ; it is a device to facilitate the making of an enlargement (or in some cases a reduction) from a drawing while maintaining the correct relative proportions and positions of the parts. Thus if some detail appears in, shall we say, the top right-hand corner of the third square from the left, second row down, it will remain in the same position in the corresponding square whatever the degree of enlargement or reduction may be. This method is very helpful if, for example, you want to make a copy of a picture in a book or magazine, provided it is permissible to rule light pencil lines on it. If, however, the picture must not be defaced, the best alternative is to rule the grid on a sheet of tracing paper, or matt celluloid, and to secure it with paper clips, or by some other means, over the picture. You can thus make use in the scenic background of any suitable material which may be at hand, without the labour of making an entirely freehand copy. For 4 mm. scale each of the squares on this drawing could represent a space of 3 in. by 3 in. ; for 7 mm. scale they might be 5 in. squares, but these suggestions can be modified to suit the particular circumstances. You can, if you wish, sub-divide the squares, so that each one becomes four, to obtain a more exact guide for the location of the various details of the drawing. Pencil lightly on the card, or whatever material is used, a grid having the same number of squares but of the required size for your scale :   3 in. or 5 in. squares, or whatever size of enlargement may have been selected. Pencil in the outline of the trees and of the shadow areas indicated by shading, using the grid lines as a guide. Cut round the skyline ; it does not matter if the edge should be a little ragged in places because foliage does not have a hard edge. If you have not been able to find a card with a satisfactory surface, use cartridge or watercolour paper and paste it to card after painting. After cutting along the skyline it will be necessary to touch up the raw edge with the appropriate colours so that it does not show up as a white line dividing land from sky.

The first wash (Fig. 50) is applied all over the card or paper and a suitable tint can be obtained by mixing permanent green middle and permanent yellow deep, all colours referred to in this chapter being from the list of Messrs. Winsor & Newton. Naturally there are plenty of other combinations which would serve equally well and I am simply mentioning those which I happen to use myself. I have found that certain colours and certain mixtures seem to be fairly satisfactory by the usual process of trial and error and that is all there is to it. The colour should be used well diluted with water for this is the highlight wash and it is important to obtain a brilliant and luminous yellow-green.   For grey surfaces, such as Essex board, Reeves' tempera colours are preferable to poster colours because they are more opaque but can be handled in much the same way. The proportions of green and yellow are a matter of individual opinion ; do not stint the yellow, however, or the result may be rather cold. Lay this first wash all over the moist card or paper as quickly and evenly as possible, and let it dry. There is, of course, no point in going over parts of the surface which it is known will be hidden by built-up foreground work. When experience has been gained you may be able to put on the second wash while the first is slightly damp and thus obtain softened outlines between the tones since the colours will run and spread a little. But that method cannot be recommended at first. The second wash then, represented by the shaded areas, will have to be applied on the dry surface, but since the areas to be covered are smaller, and the tone considerably deeper, it should not be too difficult to apply the colour reasonably evenly. Use the same two colours, named above, but a larger proportion of the green and do not thin the mixture so much with water. You can use the same brush for the larger areas, but it may be necessary to cut in quickly with a smaller one (about

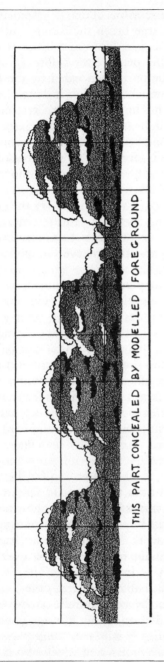

THIS PART CONCEALED BY MODELLED FOREGROUND

Fig. 50 (above)

Fig. 51 (left)

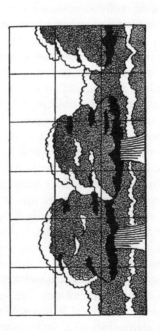

$\frac{3}{16}$ in. or $\frac{1}{4}$ in.) for some of the more tricky bits of detail. Remember that the more you can stick to the large brush the easier it will be to obtain an even wash, free from obvious blobs and brush marks. It may be necessary to strengthen the pencil lines before applying the second wash because they will be partly concealed by the first. Don't be afraid that they will be seen when the job is done ; even if pencilled in quite heavily they will not be noticed at any reasonable viewing distance. The third wash, indicated by the black areas on the drawing, is applied after the second is dry, and may be regarded as to some extent optional. It depends largely on how the backdrop will be used, and on how much it will be obscured by modelled foreground detail such as trees, buildings, etc. This time use permanent middle green and a little black. You can also try the effect of adding a little cobalt if you like, and, if you feel venturesome, put a very thin yellow wash all over one or two trees to make them a different kind of green to the others and thus relieve the monotony which is to some extent unavoidable with the simple method described here. Do not attempt to pass final judgment on any piece of work until you can try it in position on the layout and see the effect in relation to other objects *and under normal lighting conditions*. It is not unlikely that the first attempt will appear rather weak and washed out when tested in this way, but that can be discovered only by trial and error. If this should be the verdict it may be possible to save the work by strengthening the colours, but it is really better to say that the first attempt was a preliminary exercise and to start again. It is quite in order to work over oil colours but with poster colours it is apt to be an unsatisfactory business, and unsound in principle even if one may occasionally manage to get away with it in practice.

Nothing has been said about the trunks of trees, so far, because in most cases they can be concealed from view by solid foreground objects. Occasionally, however, it is impossible to avoid showing the trunks and in such cases Fig. 51 may be useful. When putting on the green washes it is advisable to work round the trunks leaving them clear, but if a little green should manage to slop over the outlines it is not likely to cause any serious trouble. The colours we use for the trunks should be sufficiently opaque to cover, and a suspicion of a green tinge would not be very harmful anyway. A suitable shade for the trunks can be made by mixing vandyke brown with white. The white will give it a grey tinge which is more suitable for most trees than pure brown and it will also confer an opaque quality. The shadows can be put in with a thin wash of cobalt, or cobalt and vandyke brown. It will be seen that the spaces between the trunks are tinted with the first and second green washes to suggest more distant masses of foliage. These also might be greyed slightly to give an effect of distance and shadow.

Our second subject may be described as a rolling downland scene, Fig. 52. This, like the tree background, is capable of considerable elaboration but is shown here in practically its simplest form. The same two colours will serve as were employed for the tree background ; permanent green middle and permanent yellow deep. It would be as well to use the colour a little thinner because the tones of grass are almost always lighter than those of the massed foliage of trees. If the reader has ever had any experience of graduated washes it would be advantageous to pin the card or paper upside down and to introduce more white while working downwards towards the skyline. This will help to produce the effect of distance. The surface should be moist for this first wash, as in the last example. For the second, or shadow, wash, indicated by shading, the same colours can be used but a little deeper in tone and with more of the green. The colour should not be quite so dark as the second wash on the tree backdrop. Most of the surface should be dry when putting in these shadow areas, but I think it will be obvious that in certain positions we should prefer a gentle gradation of tone rather than a hard line. Therefore moisten the surface at and around these places, before you start applying the paint, and gently spread and thin out the colour on the moist surface with the brush quite wet but almost empty of paint. With practice the reader will find that he can make the darker colour trail off almost imperceptibly into the lighter one, and this will help to suggest the rounded and undulating nature of the ground. It goes without saying that this graduated shading should not be employed in those cases where a shoulder or projecting spur of the ground obviously implies a hard line. Study of the drawing will, no doubt, make the point clear.

You may come to the conclusion, after considering the result, that a few shadow areas in the hollows might be deeper in tone. In that eventuality the writer ventures to suggest (although it is all horribly unorthodox) that a carbon black pencil has its uses for emphasising shadows. If used with discretion—with short light strokes—it need not entirely obscure the green tone. The result may be crude at close quarters but it will be quite satisfactory

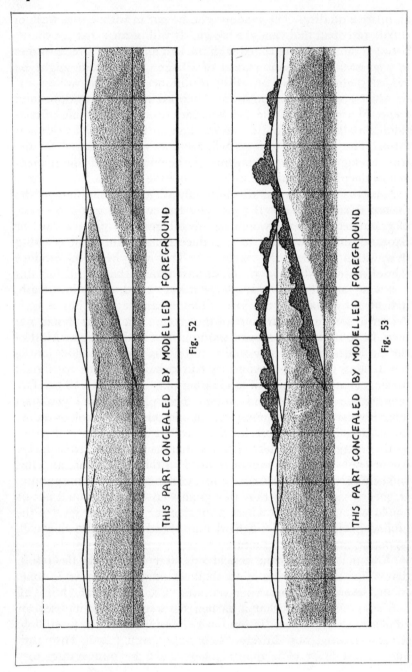

THIS PART CONCEALED BY MODELLED FOREGROUND

Fig. 52

THIS PART CONCEALED BY MODELLED FOREGROUND

Fig. 53

when the back drop is in position and seen from normal distance.

We can elaborate this downland prospect with a suggestion of distant woods and hedges something like Fig. 53. As the basis for these we may use the same green paint mixed with a little black or dark grey to give an olive tint. By this means the soft greyish green of distant trees can be suggested. Unfortunately, it is not possible to specify just how much black or white to use ; the reader must establish that by trial. If he can manage to think of relative depth of tone disassociated from colour, it may be suggested that the trees or hedges near the horizon should be only a few shades darker than the adjoining grass areas.

It is not really necessary to distinguish between light and shade because at a considerable distance colours are softened to the point where such differences of tone are hardly perceptible. There is, of course, no objection to a slight suggestion of shadow tone if the reader has progressed to the point where he feels able to undertake it, but if necessary we can get along without.

But for a hedge which is comparatively near, as shown on the right of the drawing, a rather different treatment is necessary. Because it is so much nearer than the trees on the horizon, we cannot ignore the question of light and shade. Mass in the hedge with the green, a little black, and, perhaps, a very little white. Now it will be seen that we are working partly on top of the hillside wash and for this reason the writer thinks that it may prove simpler to reverse the method we have used so far of applying highlight tones first and shadows afterwards. That is to say we put on the shadow mass first and then indicate the highlights—with dabs of colour along the top edge—by mixing white with green. This will be sufficiently opaque to enable us to impose a light tone on a dark one. The colour must be used rather dry or it may not be sufficiently opaque. Do not overdo it ; all you need is a succession of dabs and blobs, applied with a stippling motion, on the sides of the rounded masses of foliage which incline towards the presumed direction of the sun. We must, of course, use a small brush for this. If a first trial suggests that the result will be rather cold and distant, a yellow can be added or substituted for the white, or a thin wash of yellow can be flowed on after the work is dry.

Another useful background theme is a distant range of mountains with their outlines almost lost in haze. This effect can be produced with one colour wash by mixing vermilion and cobalt with the addition of a trace of white and black (light grey) to control the warmth of the resulting purple. It may be said that the more the blue predominates over the red the more distant the mountains will appear to be. The reader has probably noticed that under certain atmospheric conditions distant mountains almost merge into the sky tone ; it is an effect of this kind we are seeking. A special diagram is unnecessary as the reader can easily find photographs of mountains which will suggest typical forms. Avoid impossible mountains of the kind which suggest fairy tale illustrations, for mountains, like everything else, have definite forms governed by their structure.

Limitations of space will not permit further elaboration of the matters we have discussed in this chapter, but the simple backdrops described should cover most situations if a little ingenuity is exercised —at least as a stopgap measure—and if this chapter succeeds in giving the reader a start, from which he may hope to reach more ambitious things, it will have served its purpose. It remains to mention one or two matters which concern the use of the backdrops.

Fig. 54 shows how two backdrops can be used in combination. This is a good device to obtain an effect of distance, and if they can be separated by a space of about 1 in., as shown here, the illusion will be considerably improved. The backdrops are nailed to lengths or blocks of wood, which form solid bases and keep them apart.

In Fig. 55 the idea is developed a stage further ; there are separate tree and downland backdrops with the peaks of mountains just visible in the distance. The method of using multiple backdrops can be recommended as it is easier for the beginner to paint separate motifs on separate sheets of card or paper than to try to produce them all together. The question of relative distances will more or less look after itself if they can be arranged to stand with spaces between them as shown in these illustrations, and the depth of the baseboard required need not exceed two or three inches.

It is felt that this chapter should not close without some reference to the treatment of buildings as they form a necessary part of many landscapes. It is hoped that Fig. 56 will supply some hints which may help the reader in dealing with other scenes, either taken from pictures found in books or of his own invention. *English Villages and Hamlets*, published by Batsford, is a book which can be recommended as a valuable source of ideas for backgrounds. Although now out of print, second-hand copies may yet be obtained. Fig. 56 shows a village scene which would serve as the background for a country station. The reader need not use the whole of it, for one of the buildings might be used separately as an isolated house or farm. In view of the multi-

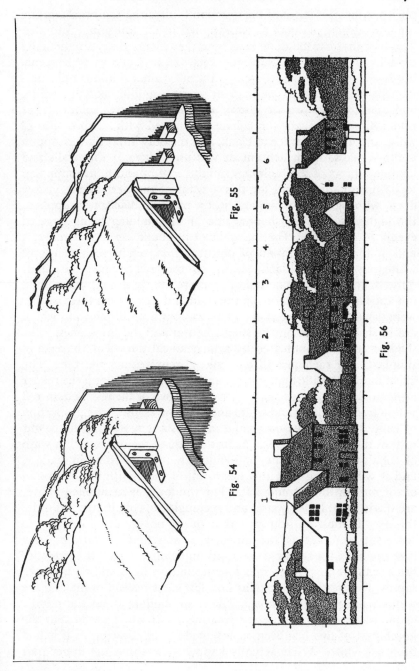

Fig. 54

Fig. 55

Fig. 56

plicity of detail it is out of the question to describe the brushwork in the same degree of detail as was applied to the foregoing examples. The best that can be done is to note the colours that were actually used by the writer to paint the various parts of this little scene. Seven colours only were used ; burnt sienna, indian red, permanent yellow deep, permanent green middle, cobalt, white, and black. They are all Winsor & Newton's poster colours. For practically every wash the colour was mixed with more or less of white and usually a trace of black, and the only important exception is the windows for which cobalt was used alone. The walls and chimney stacks of the buildings numbered 1, 5 and 6, are supposed to be cream stucco and for this a wash of the permanent yellow deep, with plenty of white and just a trace of black, was applied, the highlight and the shadow side of the building being covered evenly in one wash. For the walls of the buildings numbered 2, 3 and 4, the wash consisted of burnt sienna, again with plenty of white and very little black. Care was exercised to make the colour quite light because these buildings are relatively distant and should not appear as close as those on the right and left. When these washes were dry a very thin wash of cobalt was put over all the walls which are in shadow, both on the stucco houses and the brick ones. The shadow areas are indicated by a mechanical tint. For the sake of simplicity the roofs are all one colour, representing red tile. The effect may be a trifle monotonous and it would be better if the reader attempted to represent thatch for one or two of them. Indian red with a trace of cobalt and white and black was used, the proportion of white being increased on the most distant roofs and the colour further diluted with water. As in the case of the walls, a thin wash of cobalt was put over the roofs which are to some extent in shadow, and it will be seen that this means all of them with the exception of the one on the extreme left. The windows, as mentioned above, are made up of little squares and rectangles of cobalt, applied quite thickly. It must be admitted that this is not a very good way to represent windows as the absence of any hint of curtains may give the houses a rather empty and untenanted look. If the reader has advanced far enough in colour technique, he would do better to supply a suggestion of curtains in a few cases instead of making the window panes an even blue. The shop window about the middle of the scene requires different treatment. It will be seen that the lower part of this has been represented in the drawing as if it had been left white. What actually happened was that the upper part was washed in with cobalt, with an uneven edge which might suggest the outline of cartons and packages seen against the relative darkness inside the shop. Then a few touches of pale and diluted colour, browns, reds, and yellows, were dabbed on the white area in the lower part of the window. The space was not entirely filled ; some white was allowed to remain. This simple and rather impressionistic method of representing a shop window and its contents may sound rather odd, but the doing is really simpler than the telling and it will answer the purpose quite well. A thick line of colour, brown or green for example, can be placed above the window to represent a painted facia and a few strokes of opaque white or yellow paint will indicate the presence of lettering.

A line of shadow, made by mixing indian red and cobalt, was placed under the eaves of each house with a small pointed brush, as shown on the drawing by thick lines, and the reader can, if he likes, put similar lines just below the windows to represent the shadow cast by the sill. Alternatively, a carbon pencil could be used for this and some may find it easier to manipulate than a brush when thin lines are required. It will be seen that no chimney pots are shown in the drawing. The reader can, of course, put them in if he likes but they are not essential. Some old houses do not have them.

Doors and gates are just plane rectangles of any colour which will stand out nicely against the adjoining areas of wall. The roadway was tinted a kind of greyish fawn, made by mixing white, black, and a little permanent yellow deep.

It is hardly necessary to say much about the trees and the downs in the distance as the method of dealing with them has been described already. The trees have light and dark washes consisting of the green and yellow colours with the addition of a little white and black ; the distant downs are the same but with less of the yellow and much more of the white to produce a light toned and slightly greyed sort of green which will stand away from the colour used for the trees by reason of its coldness. The grass and hedges in the foreground are a green in which yellow predominates.

In this case it has seemed better not to project the grid lines across the drawing to avoid confusing it unnecessarily. Ticks have been placed on the marginal lines instead and the reader can join them with pencil and ruler if he wishes. The squares may be taken to represent the same area as those in Figs. 50, 52 and 53.

CHAPTER NINE

Scenic Modelling in Ultra Miniature Scales

SCENIC modelling in miniature scales, such as 2 mm. to 1 ft. or less, does not differ in essentials from work in larger scales. Since natural features such as hills and embankments are proportionately smaller it may often be more convenient to build them entirely with the earth-mix where in a larger scale a foundation structure of wood and card or wire netting would be advisable. For ground treatment materials such as sand and sawdust can be used very much as described in preceding chapters, remembering that since everything is on a smaller scale rather more delicate handling is necessary. For grass only the finest sawdust should be used or the result may appear rather coarse. Sawdust from hard woods is usually finer than that obtained from soft ones, such as deal. Perhaps a better way is to use silver sand and to paint it with matt oil colours. The coarser kind of sawdust, as usually obtained from sawmills, should be reserved for surfaces such as scrub and undergrowth. Trees can be produced from most of the materials described in Chapter Five and carpet underlay can be used for undergrowth and even for hedges if cut into narrow strips. The writer has seen scrub and bushes represented successfully with cotton wool dyed with coloured inks.

R. W. G. Bryant has made very realistic rock cliffs and outcroppings from slabs of cork. His method is to break the material and to mount it so that the irregular surfaces are displayed. Several layers can be arranged one above another to produce the required height. The cork can be coloured with poster or oil colours and the landscape is built up around it with any of the usual materials.

The same paints can be used as for larger scales, and the general technique of application will, of course, be similar. It is as well to bear in mind that a 2 mm. scale model is normally viewed from a proportionately greater scale distance than a 4 mm. one and for this reason the colours should be slightly softer and more delicate than might be considered necessary for a larger scale. The advice offered in an earlier chapter that colours used in scenic work should usually have some white or grey mixed with them is even more important when working in very small scales. Any suspicion of crudeness in the tones is sure to appear forced and artificial.

For waterways the cellophane method, described in Chapter Four, is not recommended in scales smaller than 4 mm. It is hardly possible to crumple the cellophane sufficiently to suggest anything like " scale ripples " and the effect might be more suggestive of a rough sea. It is suggested that water surfaces be painted with glossy oils—blue-green or brown—and finished with one or two coats of high-gloss transparent varnish.

Roads can be represented quite simply with matt oil paint, grey for macadam, brown for gravel, and so on. Substances such as sand should usually be avoided as in such small scales they would give the impression of an unmade road surface. Fine silver sand might be used on a rough gravel cart track and suitably painted.

A broader and more comprehensive treatment may be possible than could be contemplated in larger scales since the space at the worker's disposal is likely to be proportionately more extensive. In fact, the worker who is accustomed to a larger scale may at first encounter some difficulty in adjusting his ideas to this difference. By way of illustration we may take the case of a model farm. In 4 mm. scale, or a larger size, it is seldom possible to do much more than represent the actual farmyard and the adjoining buildings, the farmlands being of necessity confined to a more or less adequate suggestion painted on a flat backdrop. But in a scale such as 2 mm. to 1 ft. it is quite possible that space may be found for a fair representation of the agricultural lands. Similar considerations will be found to apply when modelling villages.

The construction of buildings in 2 mm. to 1 ft. scale will follow the same general lines as are employed in larger sizes, and the methods described in the writer's book, *Miniature Building Construction*, are generally applicable. It may be questioned whether it is really worth while to cut out windows and glaze them with celluloid. It will probably satisfy most workers if the window panes are painted on the card with a dark blue colour and a fine brush. The skilful worker might sometimes vary this treatment with vertical bands of a lighter colour at the sides to suggest window curtains. If, however, the windows are cut out and glazed in the usual way it is important to avoid the use of heavy card which would give the impression that the walls were unnaturally thick. Window frames are seldom set back more than $4\frac{1}{2}$ in. from the outside surface of the wall, which in 2 mm. scale is little more than 1/64 in.

It is unfortunate that no building papers are marketed for 2 mm. scale. The Merco " old stone " paper, available from Messrs. Hambling, can be used successfully, especially for massive structures such as bridges and retaining walls, and some of the tile papers will just about pass muster. It has been found that the Modelcraft brick papers do not appear noticeably disproportionate in 2 mm. scale, but some workers may prefer to tint the walls with a suitable brown or red and refrain from attempting to represent individual bricks. The writer thinks that it is quite wrong to use brown or red colour alone for brown or red brick surfaces. For brown brick it is suggested that vandyke brown or burnt umber be used with just a trace of cobalt, while for red brick indian red or burnt sienna with a trace of cobalt may be tried. In all cases a little grey may be added. It is preferable that the depth of tone should not be quite even all over ; slight patchiness and gradation will be more convincing, especially when modelling buildings which are old and weathered. Much detail which is usually modelled in 4 mm. scale would be so small that it may be omitted ; rainwater pipes and roof gutters may be taken as examples, and sunk panels on doors can be indicated by a fine pencil line (suggesting a cast shadow) on the top edge and down one side. If door panels were cut out and backed with another layer of card, as is the usual practice in larger scales, the effect might be rather coarse unless great care and patience were exercised. Chimneys can be pieces of $\frac{1}{16}$ in. dowel rod (or thick wire) glued into holes drilled in the top of the stack.

In very small scales, such as $\frac{1}{16}$ in. to 1 ft. and less, methods will not differ radically, but care must be exercised to avoid coarseness and to maintain everything in proportion. Trees in particular demand extra care. Hedges between fields might be represented by pipe cleaners, suitably dyed or painted.

A different form of construction is usually employed for buildings ; they are shaped in the solid from stripwood of various sizes and for buildings of complex form, with wings and gables, two or more pieces of different dimensions are glued together. Roofs are formed by shaping the wood to give a suitable pitch with a small plane or a knife. Another, and quicker method, is to glue a piece of triangular section stripwood on top of the main block. The shapes thus formed can be covered with a watercolour paper, a single piece being bent round over the roof and sides if desired. The ends must be covered with separate pieces cut to shape. The buildings are tinted with poster or water colours, only the most significant and easily distinguished details being shown. It goes without saying that no attempt will be made to distinguish individual tiles or bricks. Windows may be represented by a rectangle of dark blue and few workers will feel disposed to show details of the frame or sashing, which would probably be out of scale in any case. A fine pencil line might be drawn just below the window to suggest the shadow cast by the sill. Doors, similarly, need be nothing more than an upright rectangle of colour, but in certain cases a tiny strip of card might be glued above to represent a hood.

Some workers may prefer to work direct on the wood block with matt *oil* colours, omitting the paper covering. It would be advisable to treat the end grains with a good wood filler first.

Chimney stacks can be made from strips of fine stripwood, $\frac{1}{16}$ in. by $\frac{1}{8}$ in. being a useful size for the purpose, but the chimney pots should be left to the imagination in so small a scale.